THE SHELF BOOK

Complete Do-It-Yourself Systems for Building Shelves in
Living Rooms, Kitchens, Closets, Basements, Garages, Etc.

THE SHELF BOOK

Complete Do-It-Yourself Systems for Building Shelves in
Living Rooms, Kitchens, Closets, Basements, Garages, Etc.

Written and Illustrated by
Jon M. Zegel

Running Press
Philadelphia, Pennsylvania

International representatives: Kaimon & Polon, Inc.,
2175 Lemoine Avenue, Fort Lee, New Jersey 07024

Printed in the United States of America

Library of Congress Cataloging in Publication Data
Zegel, Jon, 1948-
   The Shelf Book.
   Bibliography: p. 135
   Includes index.
   1. Shelving (for books)   2. Storage in the home.
I. Title.
TT197.5.B6Z43   684.1'6   77-12366
ISBN 0-89471-000-1 Paperback
ISBN 0-89471-001-X Library binding

Typography: Stymie, by CompArt, Philadelphia, Pennsylvania

Cover design by Jim Wilson
Cover illustration by Verlin Miller
Back cover photography by Kas Schlots
Interior design by Fetterman & Fetterman
Editor: Peter J. Dorman

Running Press
38 South Nineteenth Street
Philadelphia, Pennsylvania 19103

Premise

I wrote *The Shelf Book* to give you a working, practical knowledge of the various hardware, materials, and techniques of shelf building.

Since it would be impossible to write a book that solves every shelving problem anyone might ever encounter, the focus is on showing how to create your own solutions and how to execute them using any one or a combination of the methods described. The emphasis is on the practical as well as the aesthetic.

Following the line of reasoning that is less practical to feed a man than teach him to fish, I have written this book to give you the information you need to use your ingenuity, talents, and creativity in order to solve your present and future shelving needs.

Contents

Read This First: Terms & Tools

This is a book about shelves and shelving. <u>Yawn</u>. Trouble is that a lot of people need shelving. Fact is that shelving built and/or installed by professionals is expensive, often very expensive.

Yet, another fact is that the construction of shelving is simple once you understand the basics, and not beyond the reach of anyone who can do simple tasks with hand tools. Some projects require no tools at all. If a particular project requires more extensive experience or costly tools, I'll try to offer suggestions of inexpensive ways to have the work done by someone with the experience or tools should you choose not to get too deeply into the construction. Quite beautiful results can be achieved at lesser costs by combining your work and the work of others.

There is a ratio here to understand: the more of the work you do yourself, the less the project will cost. Since people are paid for their labor, you can spend less out of pocket by doing the work yourself. This does not consider the cost of *your* time—but we'll assume that you are willing to "donate" it.

Cost aside, many people, myself included, get great satisfaction from designing and building things around their home or office.

The purpose of my writing this book is to create a central source of ideas and techniques. It is by no means all- inclusive; but I have tried to organize it so that a person who knows nothing about building can acquire enough understanding of the basics to be *successful* in a shelf- building project. I have also included some projects for people with more experience, and some for those in between.

Beyond that, it has been my aim to cover the subject well enough that when you finish the book you will be able to construct more sophisticated shelves than you thought you could when you started reading it.

Part One of *The Shelf Book* treats materials and techniques that are needed to build the projects described later on. And since all shelves that you build yourself or even assemble from premade components are "custom" to some degree, I have tried to outline the factors to consider in creating a workable design.

Part Two deals with shelving that is "half and half," that is, where you use prefabricated hardware, premade shelves, or complete kits. Your half is the assembly or installation; the other half is done for you.

Part Three considers shelves and shelf systems that you build completely yourself, using wood, Plexiglas, glass, metal, and other materials. I have tried to arrange these in order of increasing sophistication.

Part Four shows some shelves for specific applications or for specific areas around the house. I have put them in a section all to themselves since they are much more specialized than those shown in Parts Two or Three.

Part Five concerns things to add to your shelving systems to make them more beautiful, or useful, or both. You can really increase the utility of your shelves by adding things specifically designed for your storage and general living situations.

Part Six includes some sources of additional information and a glossary of terms. *I urge you to use the glossary.* Anything, no matter how complex, can be most clearly understood by breaking it down into small understandable parts, understanding each part, and then putting back those parts into an understandable whole. Since words comprise the smallest parts of a book, first clarify the words if you have difficulty understanding something. It should then come into focus for you.

BASIC TERMS

With that in mind, let's cover a few of the terms I know you will encounter and that I have defined or used in a special way.

Shelf: a horizontal, flat piece of wood, metal, glass, plastic, etc., used to store or display things.

Upright: the vertical support for a shelf or shelves.

Unit: an assembly consisting of two uprights supporting one or more shelves.

System: this word is used in two ways. (1) A method of building or assembling; the "pipe system" would be shelves assembled using pipe. (2) Two or more units put together to make a more complex or larger area of shelves; e.g., a "wall system."

A WORD ABOUT TOOLS

You have probably heard the maxim, "It's a poor craftsman that blames his tools." Do you know why? It is because a real craftsman *has* the right tools for the job. The point is that your investment in tools will pay great dividends in the appearance of the completed project. That is not to say that you should run out and spend hundreds of dollars on tools. But it is to say that the right tools will save you time and energy. Tools can also be borrowed or rented; so if cash is in short supply, explore one of these alternatives as well.

Most of the projects in this book require only the most basic hand tools—a saw, screwdriver, electric drill, a hammer, etc. Some do require a special tool or two, which I will note as we go along. I will always try to offer alternatives to the tools specified, cheaper sources, or someone already equipped whom you can get to do part of the job for you.

I have accumulated a nice selection of tools by buying those needed for each specific project I get into around the house. For each project I take on now, there is less of a need to buy or borrow tools—I even did one job recently when I didn't need to buy any. If I compare what I would have had to pay for professional services to my cost of materials (not including my time), the savings have more than paid for my tools—they have been paid for several times over.

* * *

To get the most out of this book, read it straight through Part One, and then scan through the various projects and select ones that will be the most useful to you. I wish you great success.

Part One
Basics

Materials

Here I will discuss materials that can be used for making shelves. I won't pretend to give a complete listing, but rather to cover the most commonly used materials and those you will have the easiest time finding. There are many other materials available and some variations of the materials mentioned, so you need not be limited to only those mentioned.

WOOD

There are four types of wood most often used in building shelving. They are pine, plywood, particle board (composition board, flake board), and solid hardwoods.

Pine

Pine is a popular material because it comes in convenient lengths and widths and thicknesses for building shelves. "Standard shelving pine," also called "1 by 12," is the most widely used. Its actual measurements are 3/4 inch thick by 11-1/4 inches wide—the finished size after the lumber has been milled. Besides the 11-1/4 inch width, "one by" pine shelving also comes in 4 inch, 6 inch, 8 inch, and 10 inch widths, and occasionally 14 inch. Lengths available run from 6 feet to 16 feet in two foot increments. Virtually every lumberyard carries some of these sizes; most carry all of them.

"One by two" pine (actually 3/4 inch by 1-1/2 inches) has many applications in shelf building, from making supports to creating faces on the edges of shelves. Applications will be covered as they come up.

Pine, a softwood, works easily with hand tools and takes paint, stains, and other finishes well. Pine can also take laminates; but since it is usually more expensive than plywood, it is more economical to use the latter for laminating.

The quality of the actual wood is variable, so a system of grades has been established. The two most commonly found grades are *#1 grade," C" or better,* and *standard #2 grade.*

Grade #1, "C" or better, is the superior grade of the two. It allows pin knots (very tiny knots) that are all but invisible; and it will be clearer and straighter than #2. Grade #1 is more expensive than #2, but will make a better product *if* knots are objectionable. Also, since the area around a knot is not quite so strong as the rest of the board, #1 grade tends to be a little stronger in general.

Grade #2, a rougher pine than #1, allows tight knots (those not likely to come loose). This grade will cost less than #1 and, if you enjoy knotty pine, you will appreciate its appearance. Economically, this grade is a good choice if you will be painting. What you will have to do, however, is to seal the knots to prevent sap from seeping through the paint. This is done by giving each knot and a small area around it a thorough coat of white shellac. Allow this to dry thoroughly before painting.

In the area where I live, the prices compare like this: about 45 cents per foot for 1 × 12 grade #2; about $1.00 per foot for the same in grade #1.

Pine is also available in other sizes. "Two by" pine is pine that, before milling, is 2 inches thick by 2, 4, 6, 8, 10, or 12 inches wide. The after-milling sizes, naturally, will be somewhat smaller.

"Two by" material is used for strong uprights, very strong shelves, or as supports. It is ideal for use as utility shelves because of its resistance to sag under great weight, but can be beautiful in decorative applications because of its bulk and rugged appearance.

When you go to the lumberyard or building supply store to select your pine, here are a few things to look for.

Warping is the tendency of wood to bend and it is caused by improper drying and/or storage. Wood can bend along the length (bow, twist), or across the width (cup). The less the wood is warped, the easier it is to work with; so look the pieces over carefully before selecting. Sight along the length of the board and examine each of the four lengthwise edges. The straighter the board the better. Also examine the end of the board to check for cupping. Do not expect to find pieces that are perfectly straight or completely free from defects— there is no such thing. But don't be afraid to be selective. Pick the best pieces the dealer has; they are the same price as the warped ones.

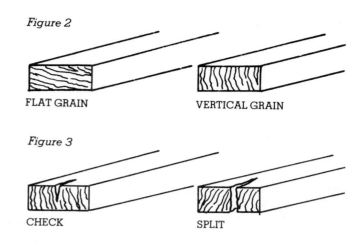

Figure 2

FLAT GRAIN   VERTICAL GRAIN

Figure 3

CHECK   SPLIT

Figure 1

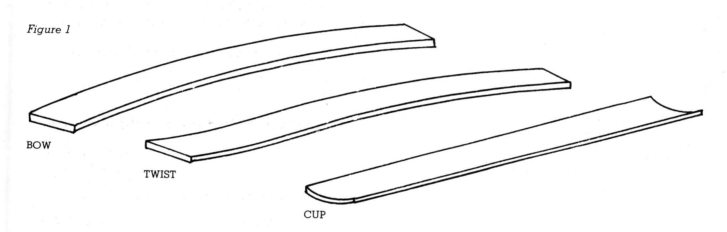

BOW

TWIST

CUP

Another factor to check is whether the piece is *flat grain* or *vertical grain.* Figure 2 shows the difference. Vertical grain is generally preferable to flat grain because it is more resistant to warping from moisture. However, do not reject a straight piece that is flat grained because of this characteristic alone. If it is an otherwise suitable piece, take it. If there is an equal piece that is vertical grained, select it in preference. (See Fig. 2.)

Look the piece over for *splits, checks* (splits that do not go all the way through the board), and pieces broken out of the edges. These are reasons for rejecting a piece also. (See Fig. 3.)

Splits or checks that are very near the end of an otherwise suitable board should be cut off before using. Nails or screws driven into the checked or split area will often cause more splits; yet the area beyond the split is usually sound.

Plywood

Plywood is composed of thin layers of wood laminated to one another with a strong glue. The direction of the grain alternates from layer to layer, making the finished sheet very strong and resistant to bending and warping. Plywood comes in thicknesses of 1/4, 3/8, 1/2, 5/8, and 3/4 inches. It is most often sold in 4-by-8-foot sheets, but some dealers sell half-sheets (4 by 4). For shelving with a span of 3 feet or more, I recommend 5/8 or 3/4 inch plywood; the selection between the two should be determined by the weight to be supported. If there is any question, use the 3/4". (See Fig. 4.)

The quality grades for plywood are a bit more complex than for pine, but they are easy to understand. First, there are two basic divisions in plywood: *interior* (Int), for use indoors where moisture is not a problem; and *exterior* (Ext), for use outdoors and indoors where moisture is present, like in a basement or bathroom. The difference is not so much in the wood as in the glue used to hold the layers together.

Plywood is graded by the quality of its outside layers of wood. It is graded by letters from A (best) to D (worst). "A" is the best, close-grained and smooth. "B" is also smooth, but plugs (pieces inserted to fill a defect) are allowed. "C" and "D" are rougher grades, where the faces can be pieced together and knots left in place rather than plugged.

Figure 4

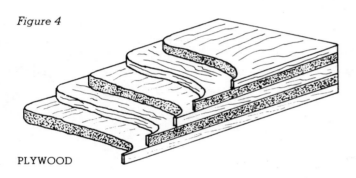

PLYWOOD

Since a piece of plywood has two sides, the grade for each piece has two letters. Not all combinations are available or useful, but I'll list the most common ones:

A-A Int or Ext: both sides perfect.

A-B Int or Ext: one side perfect, one side plugged.

A-C Ext and A-D Int: one side perfect, one side construction grade.

B-B Int or Ext: both sides smooth, neither perfect.

The choice you make will be determined by the application you have in mind. Be sure to look the grades over at the yard. The grades given above are from the American Plywood Association, but some manufacturers use their own systems. And just as with pine, be selective.

Plywood is also available with special veneers like birch, maple, amesica, etc. They can be rather dif-

ficult to find and order, but if you have a project that would benefit from a good veneer, your dealer may be able to suggest a source or order it for you if he does not stock it.

Plywood takes wood and plastic laminates well, and can be finished with paint, stain, or any of the clear finishes. It is, after all, real wood.

A difficulty that can be encountered with plywood is that gaps may be discovered in the inside layers during cutting. There are two solutions to this. One is to select what is called "finnish" plywood, specially made to have no gaps. The second is to fill any gaps with wood filler and sand it smooth.

To make shelving from plywood, it is often necessary to make long, straight cuts. A table saw, circular saw, or radial arm saw is ideal, but the cuts can be made with a hand saw or a sabre saw (electric jig saw). With a sabre saw, it is advantageous to use a simple helper to guide the saw straight. The helper is made from a long, straight board clamped to the board to be cut with two C-clamps. The sole plate or foot of the sabre saw rides along the straightedge, thus keeping it from veering off course. In laying out your cuts, it is better to have the grain running the length of the shelf. (See Fig. 5.)

An alternative to making the long cuts yourself is to have your lumber dealer make them. There will probably be a small charge for doing it; but if you are uncertain of your ability to make the cuts yourself, the extra investment will be well worth it.

Particle board (composition board, flake board)

Particle board, also known as composition board or flake board, is made of small chips or flakes of wood mixed with a bonding material which is then pressed and heat- treated to form sheets. It is very dense and thus quite heavy compared to pine. It is very resistant to warping and almost never cups. Almost all lumberyards and building supply yards sell it.

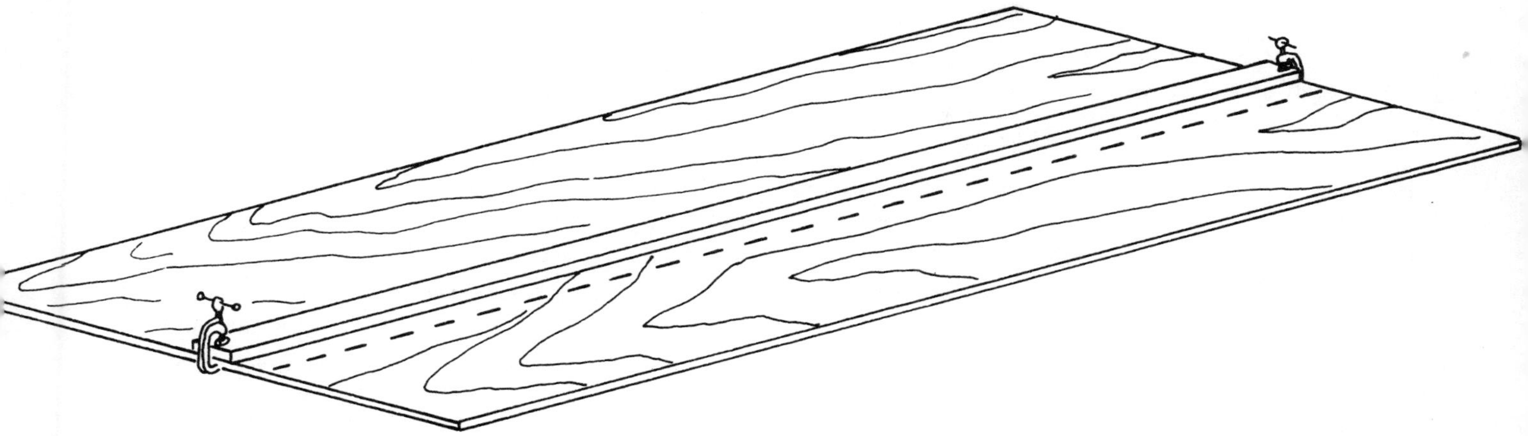

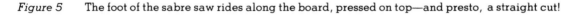

Figure 5   The foot of the sabre saw rides along the board, pressed on top—and presto, a straight cut!

Particle board, like plywood, comes in 4-by-8-foot sheets and in the same thicknesses as plywood (see page 13.) It can be cut and worked just like plywood and accepts paints and laminates well. It can also be stained and finished like solid wood, but stain will not hide its appearance. Many people, however, really like the look of the composition materials, a look that will be enhanced by stain and finishes.

Spans of more than 4 feet are not workable with these materials because they will tend to sag under their own weight. So keep spans of particle board to 3-1/2 feet or less.

Solid hardwood

Hardwoods are available in many varieties, including oak, maple, cherry, walnut, birch, and mahogany. Hardwoods are the most expensive of the shelving materials described here, and can be the most difficult to locate. Many lumber dealers do not wish to invest the money necessary to stock a full line of these; and their scarcity in nature complicates the matter. But hardwoods will produce a beautiful product. They are a little more difficult to work with, but they take stains, finishes, and tung oil beautifully.

Hardwoods are available in a variety of

thicknesses, the most readily available being 1/2 inch and 3/4 inch.

Widths and lengths are the same as for board pine (see page 17), but few yards carry a complete selection. Hardwoods also are available in the "two by" sizes.

Keep in mind that you can use 1/2-inch hardwood where you would ordinarily use 3/4-inch plywood because the hardwoods are much stronger.

PLEXIGLAS

Plexiglas, the Rohm and Haas trademark for acrylic sheet, is a flexible plastic material that comes in many shapes and colors. I'll use the term plexi or Plexiglas rather than acrylic sheet because it is well known and understood. But there are other manufacturers of acrylic sheet, and I have no particular preference for one manufacturer or another.

You will find plexi in sheets ranging in thickness from 1/8 inch to 3/4 inch. One-fourth inch is the most popular and available thickness. Sheet sizes are variable, but can be found in up to 4 by 8 feet. Most dealers either stock smaller sheets or will cut a sheet down for you so that you won't be forced to buy a lot more than you need. Plexi is also available in hollow tubes, blocks, and round and square rods or bars. Colors generally available are clear, smoked (gray or brown), black, and white. Less common colors are red, blue, yellow, green, and mirror.

Plexiglas is a soft material that can be worked with regular hand tools as well as the most common power tools. It can be sanded, cut, drilled, and bent. Following is a list of tools you may need for projects with Plexiglas. Not all tools would be needed for all projects.

Cutting tools:
Scriber (plastic cutting tool) for 1/8 and 1/4 inch.
Special blade for circular saw.
Special blade for sabre saw.
Coping saw, fine blade (for curved cuts).

Drilling:
Sharp, high-speed twist drills.

Bending:
Strip heater (Briskeat R-36 or similar), less than $12.

Cementing:
Acrylic solvent plus applicator (general use).
Thickened acrylic cement (high strength and outdoor use).

Polishing and edge finishing:
Buffing kit (muslin wheel for electric drill, polishing compound for plexi).
"Wet or Dry" sandpaper, 400 and 600 grit.

Keep in mind, though, that many plexi dealers for the do-it-yourselfer will cut, polish, and do a lot of the other work for you. There will be a charge for it, of course. But don't be afraid of plexi. It is not hard to work with, and a little practice will show you the great results you can get.

Because Plexiglas is soft, it will scratch quite easily. Fortunatley, the scratches are not difficult to remove or hide. Auto paste wax applied and buffed will conceal light surface scratches. Deeper scratches can be rubbed out using regular toothpaste. Deeper ones yet can be buffed out using the buffing kit.

Cutting

Cutting operations will vary with the thickness of the material and according to whether the cuts are straight or curved.

To make straight cuts in plexi 1/4 inch thick or thinner, use a scriber to scratch the line of the cut into the plexi itself. Then with the scribed line facing up, place a piece of 3/4″ dowel under the line and press down on both sides of the line about 2 inches away. The plexi will break quite cleanly. This method is not usable for cuts that are closer than 1-1/2 inches from the edge of the piece, since there wouldn't be room enough to push.

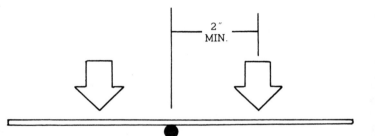

Figure 6 The scribe-and-break method of cutting plexi.

For straight cuts in the thicker plexi, or for cuts too close to the edge for the scriber, you can use a hand or power saw.

A fine-toothed hand saw will make clean cuts. Be sure that the blade is sharp; take long, even strokes, letting the saw do the work. Don't add any extra pressure or force the work.

A circular saw, table saw, or radial arm saw, with a carbide tipped plywood blade or a special plexi blade, will make great cuts. The blade should have a minimum of 6 teeth per inch and needs to be sharp. Smoothy push the saw or feed the plexi to the blade smoothly: *never force it.* Leave the paper backing on the plexi while cutting.

A sabre saw with a blade of not less than 14 teeth per inch can be used for straight or curved cuts. For straight cuts, clamp a straightedge guide to the saw to keep the blade from veering off the line. For curved cuts, simply follow your marked line. As with the other methods, leave the backing on the plexi and feed smoothly; do not force.

A coping saw with a fine blade can also be used for curved cuts. As before, feed smoothly and evenly. A coping saw cut will require a little more sanding than usual to make edges perfectly smooth, because the saw marks will be left behind.

Drilling

Drilling in plexi requires some special attention, but the operation is not difficult. The underside of the material where the drill will come out is subject to chipping and cracking around the hole. To prevent this, slow the rate at which you are feeding the drill into the plexi as you approach the point of breaking through.

The drilling can be done with either a hand or an electric drill. Ordinary high-speed twist drills like the ones used for metal are suitable, as long as they are sharp. The plexi should be backed with a piece of soft wood to help prevent chipping as the drill bit exits.

Electric drilling for holes up to 3/8 inch should be done at high speed (approximately 3000 RPM). For sizes larger than 3/8 inch, drilling is done at a slower speed to make a cleaner hole. If you don't

have a variable speed drill, you can accomplish the same effect as the lower speed by pulsing the drill off and on, particularly as the drill is about to exit the material. A light, even pressure in all electric drilling of plexi will give the best results.

If you will be drilling with a hand drill, securing the plexi down to the work surface is important. As before, back the hole with a piece of soft wood, and clamp the whole assembly down. Drill very slowly with a light, even pressure. Too much pressure will cause the back side of the hole to chip. The sharper the bits the better.

Bending

Bending of clear, smoked, and colored plexi is done using a device called a *strip heater*. Never try to bend plexi using a stove, open flame, etc. Plexi will burn if exposed to too high a heat, and if heated too much will drip. If you have ever gotten a drop of candle wax on your hand, you have only a small idea of the pain of a drop of melted plexi; it is more than twice as hot, and it sticks—so don't do it, OK? Bending is made possible by the strip heater's heating a very narrow portion of the plexi along the line of the intended bend. (Note: Although mirror plexi can be bent, I have had uniformly poor results trying to bend it. The mirror surface is almost always destroyed or distorted along the bend and in the area around it.)

Figure 7 Bending plexi with a strip heater.

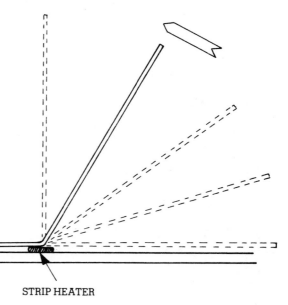

STRIP HEATER

When using the strip heater, remove the protective paper on the plexi. Mark the line of your bend with a grease pencil or china marker. Place the plexi over the strip heater along the line of the bend such that you will be bending it up toward you. The heating must be thorough. For 1/4-inch plexi, this will take around 12 minutes. As you bend, keep the material over the heater. After the bend is made, remove the material from the heater and hold it in position until cool. (See Fig. 7.)

Bending produces a radiused joint, i.e., a joint with a rounded corner. For a perfectly square corner, two flat pieces are glued together.

Figure 8

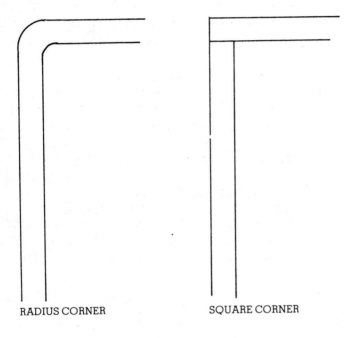

RADIUS CORNER   SQUARE CORNER

Cementing

There are two types of "glues" for Plexiglas. *Solvent* is a water-thin liquid and is a chemical that melts the two pieces of plexi together. In using solvent, follow these guidelines: The edges to be joined should be smooth and sanded (not polished), and should fit squarely. Test-fit the parts and make any adjustments needed. Remove the protective paper and assemble the joint, using masking tape to hold the pieces together. Read and follow any special recommendations on the solvent can. Apply

the solvent with a syringe, a special applicator, or a drawing pen. Apply it sparingly—use just enough to fill the joint, but not enough to spill beyond it. (Solvent spilled on the surface will mar it; the blemishes can be removed by sanding with wet and dry sandpaper and polishing.) The joint should be allowed to dry thoroughly.

The other glue for plexi is a *thickened cement.* This glue is about as thick as, say, Vaseline® and is applied in much the same way as any glue. Thickened cement takes longer to set but produces a joint with higher strength and better resistance to weather than solvent joints.

To join plexi with cement, the edges should be "satin finish" (see below), but not polished. Remove the protective paper and check the parts for a good fit. A small bead of cement along the edge of the parts to be joined is adequate. Join the pieces gently and clamp or hold them together until the joint sets; and then allow the cement to dry thoroughly undisturbed. Drying times vary from one manufacturer to another, but they average around two hours. Check the tube for the exact drying time of the cement you are using.

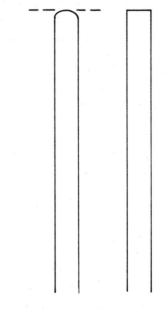

Figure 9   When finishing edges, keep ends square.

Polishing and edge finishing

Polishing and edge finishing was always a mystery to me until I tried it. It's not hard at all.

In finishing edges, it is best to work toward keeping the edges square rather than allowing them to be rounded off. If you try to join edges that have been rounded off, the joint will be less strong than if the edges had been square, and bubbles will form in the joint. (See Fig. 9.)

There are three stages of finish. Since, to get to the last you pass through the first two, we'll take them in sequence.

(1) The first stage is a "smooth edge." This is an unpolished edge where saw marks or other cutting marks have been removed. A smooth edge is made by filing out deep marks with a medium-fine metal file and sanding with a medium-grit sandpaper. The same result can be created by drag-ging a knife blade along the edge like a scraper. Finishing up with a little sanding is usually needed.

(2) The second stage is "satin finish." This stage, after the smooth finish, is made by sanding the edge with 400-or 600-grit "wet and dry" sandpaper. Using the "wet and dry" with a little water works best, as it helps keep the paper from clogging up with plastic and aids smoothing at the same time.

(3) In the third stage, "polished edges" are made by buffing a satin edge with a muslin buffing wheel and fine-grit buffing compound. This will produce an edge as clear and bright as the surface. Follow the instructions on the buffing compound.

It's a good idea to look over the pamphlets offered by the manufacturers. You'll find these in stores that sell plexi; also, you can send for them using the addresses in the back of this book.

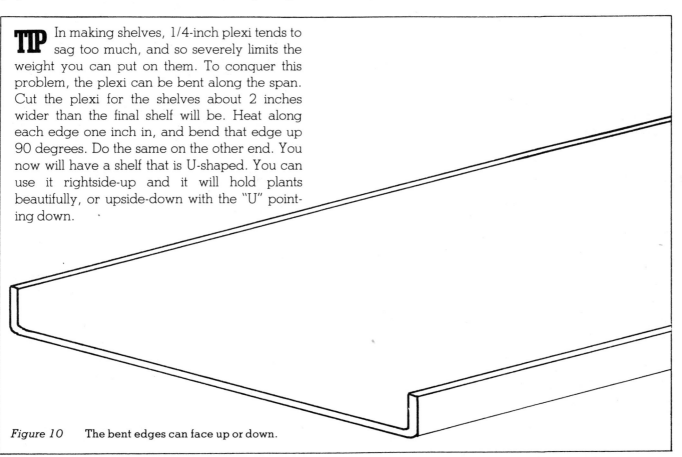

TIP In making shelves, 1/4-inch plexi tends to sag too much, and so severely limits the weight you can put on them. To conquer this problem, the plexi can be bent along the span. Cut the plexi for the shelves about 2 inches wider than the final shelf will be. Heat along each edge one inch in, and bend that edge up 90 degrees. Do the same on the other end. You now will have a shelf that is U-shaped. You can use it rightside-up and it will hold plants beautifully, or upside-down with the "U" pointing down.

Figure 10   The bent edges can face up or down.

PLASTIC PIPE

Plastic pipe is becoming a popular material for both do-it-yourselfers and professionals because it is easy to work and much cheaper than copper or brass.

Plastic pipe is made of PVC (polyvinyl chloride). It is strong and lightweight and can be worked with the same tools which are used for soft metals and wood.

The pieces of pipe are assembled with plastic fit-tings that come in the usual shapes: L, T, X, and others. The pipe and fittings are assembled using a special solvent that melts the pieces together. (See Fig. 11.)

A more complete description of exactly how to work with plastic pipe is found in the section called "Pipe System," beginning on page 50.

Plastic pipe can be purchased at building supply stores, home improvement centers, plumbing supply stores, and larger hardware stores.

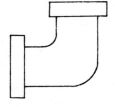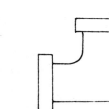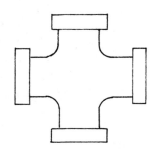

Figure 11   Pipe fittings.

Fastening and Hanging

FASTENING WOOD TOGETHER

I'm lazy. I hate to drive nails or screws if I don't have to. But there are times when they are needed, so we'll talk a bit about them here.

Screws and screwdriving

Wood screws are stronger and more permanent than nails. They have threads or teeth that bite into the wood to get a grip.

Figure 12

FLAT-HEAD WOOD SCREW

ROUND-HEAD WOOD SCREW

OVAL-HEAD WOOD SCREW

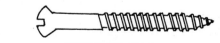

LAG SCREW

Wood screws are sized by two numbers: one that tells the length in inches and one that tells the diameter. Diameters run from 0 to 14; the higher the number, the thicker the screw. The numbers correspond *roughly* to 64ths of an inch. For example, a No. 8 screw would be approximately 1/8 inch in diameter (8/64 = 1/8). Lengths available vary with diameter, but run generally from 1/2 inch to 6 inches in increments of one half inch.

Wood screws are available in three head shapes: flat head, oval head, and round head. Flat heads are made to recess into the wood and not extend beyond the surface. Oval head screws are used for attaching moldings and other materials where a little bit of head showing makes the installation look neat. Round head screws are used when you want the head to show completely, and often to hold other materials to wood, as the head's shoulder fits flat on the surface being held. Round heads are also used when the wood is thin and any recess cut for a flat or oval head screw would weaken the surface.

When using flat head screws, a recess called a countersink is made to allow the screws to fit flush with the material's surface. There are three tools that can be used for this task. The first is a pilot bit, a special tool just for flat head screws that drills a pilot hole (see below) and makes the countersink all at one time. These are sold by the diameter of each screw. (See Fig. 13.)

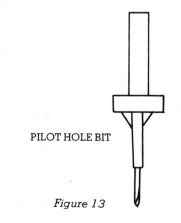

PILOT HOLE BIT

Figure 13

The second tool is called a countersink. It is a special drill bit for cutting the recess. It will work for all screw sizes because the size of the recess is determined by how far you push the countersink into the wood.

The third is more of a trick than a special tool. With a drill bit that is nearly the same size as the screw head, drill a very short distance into the wood. This will create a recess. The danger here is going too far—so use a light touch.

Driving wood screws can be made a lot easier with less risk of splitting or cracking the wood if a "pilot hole" is used. A pilot hole is a hole drilled in the wood or other material that is smaller in diameter than the shank of the screw and that removes some of the wood that the screw would have had to pass through, yet leaves enough wood for the screw to get a solid bite. The pilot hole chart (Fig. 14) will give you the correct sizes to drill pilot holes in soft and hard woods. The sizes for soft woods are a bit smaller than for hardwoods because leaving a little extra material helps the screw grip better in the softer woods. (See Fig. 14.)

The correct size screwdriver is an important factor in getting satisfactory results with screws. The blade of the screwdriver should be the same width as the slot and the same length. If the blade is thinner or longer or shorter the screw slot can be burred or destroyed, making driving difficult and removal impossible. Also, the wrong size screwdriver will more easily slide out of the slot and mar the surface of your work. (See Fig. 15.)

For screws larger than No. 14, a "lag bolt" or "lag screw" is used. Lag screws have square or hexagonal heads and are much larger than wood screws, with diameters from 1/4 inch to 1/2 inch (in 1/16-inch increments) and with lengths from 2 to 12 and sometimes 14 inches.

In choosing the length and diameter of a screw, common sense is your best bet. Consult your hardware person for advice. One tip I can offer: If you are joining two pieces of wood together, choose a screw size such that the threads of the screw have a bite in both pieces of wood. (See Fig. 16.)

Figure 14 **PILOT HOLE CHART**

Wood-Screw Size	Drill size for Hardwood	Drill size for Softwood
No. 0	1/32	1/32
1	3/64	1/32
3	1/16	3/64
4	1/16	3/64
5	5/64	1/16
6	3/32	1/16
7	3/32	5/64
8	7/64	5/64
9	1/8	3/32
10	1/8	3/32
11	1/8	3/32
12	9/64	7/64
14	9/64	7/64

(Chart adapted from Sears/Craftsman power tool accessories, Sears Roebuck and Co. and Simpsons-Sears Limited.)

Figure 15   Screwdriver should fit the slot in the screw.

Wood screws and lag bolts will drive much more easily if the threads are rubbed with a piece of ordinary bar soap. I save the pieces that are too small for the shower in a small plastic bag in my tool box. I told you before that I am lazy, and I never drive a screw without the soap. Try it, you'll be surprised at the difference.

To use nails correctly, understanding the direction of forces is the key. Simply put, the nail will hold as long as there is not force pushing the nail out. Nails will hold against forces applied from almost any angle except a force that is exactly opposite to the direction it was driven in.

Figure 16

Figure 17

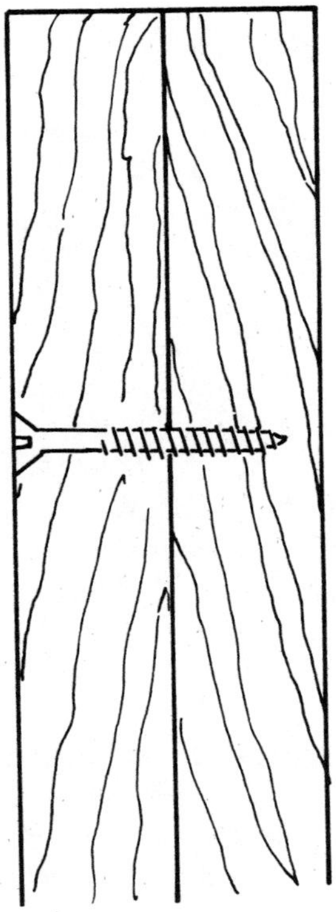

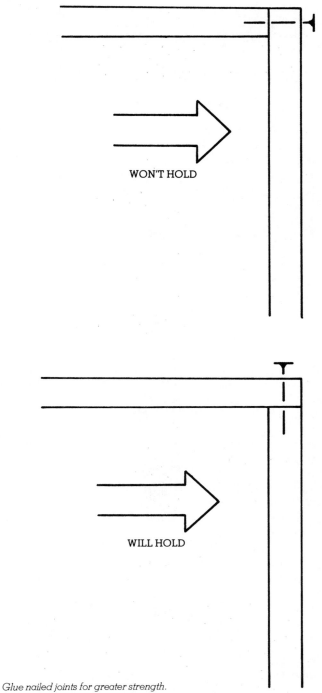

Threads grip into both pieces of wood.

Nails and nailing

Nails hold wood together by friction. They have no threads or teeth to bite into the wood. (There is an exception to this: flooring nails and some other special-application nails have small ridges along their lengths.) But fear not, if you live in a wood house—almost all of your house is held up with nails, for they do have considerable holding power. The key is to use nails correctly; improperly driven, they won't hold.

Glue nailed joints for greater strength.

Vibration will also work nails loose. So if you are making a project for a van or a mobile home, etc., choose screws.

For our purposes, there are basically two types of nails: headed, or common, nails and unheaded, or finishing, nails.

Figure 18

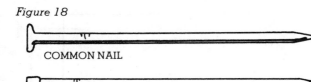

COMMON NAIL

FINISHING NAIL

The headed or common nail is the workhorse of nails. They are the strongest nails and are available in sizes from about 1 inch to 10 inches in length. They are used for basic construction and where heads showing won't make a difference.

Figure 19

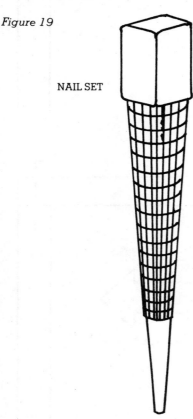

NAIL SET

Unheaded or finishing nails are used for construction and for finishing a project where a visible nail head would be objectionable. Because these nails are headless, they can be driven slightly below the

surface of the wood and the hole left can be filled with wood filler. There is a special tool for driving these nails below the surface (called "setting"). The tool, called a *nail set,* is a steel tool designed for this job. (See Fig. 19.)

Note: if you will be staining your project, consult the package for the wood filler. Some fillers, once dried, will not take stain; so the stain may be mixed with the filler before the hole is filled, or a pre-stained wood filler may be purchased.

Glues and gluing

Glues for wood are useful to the builder. There are two types that I will cover here. There are others, but these will do 99% of all gluing jobs for projects in this book.

The first type is white glue (Elmer's, Soho, etc.), and it is my favorite for wood. It is strong and waterproof when dry, but cleans up with water before dry. It takes several hours to set and about 12 hours until fully dry. But once dry it is nearly indestructible. It is used where two pieces of wood are joined together, even if nails or screws are used. It gives extra protection from stress and vibration.

The other glue is contact cement. This cement is applied to both surfaces and allowed to dry; then the pieces are joined together. Once the pieces have been joined, that's it. They are together for good. So if the pieces you are joining may need to be moved about or fiddled a bit, use white glue if possible. If not, do all your fitting and fiddling ahead of time, then join with the contact cement.

Contact cement is used most often for laminating, such as applying Formica® (laminated plastic) or veneers, or for joining two large surfaces together (like two pieces of plywood to make one piece twice as thick).

In the past, the liability of contact cement has been dangerous fumes and extreme flammability. There is a new product, however, that is a water-based contact cement. No fumes and no fire hazard. And it works just as well as the old type. Choose the water-based type if you can.

As with all products, follow the manufacturer's instructions for use and surface preparation. You will be rewarded by the product's doing what it is supposed to do.

FASTENING TO WALLS OR CEILINGS

How to find a stud

Walls that are covered by plaster or plasterboard or drywall are supported by vertical 2 × 4's called studs. When you are putting up something heavy, screws or nails driven into these studs will give much more solid support than will the same fasteners in the plaster or drywall. This is because plaster and similar materials will tend to crumble or crack under the stress, whereas the wood 2 × 4's will hold solidly.

But finding a stud can be tricky since we can't see through the plaster to the studs behind. So here are three methods for finding studs. Each one used on its own will work; using two in combination is *almost* foolproof.

(1) The first method is measuring. Luckily, studs are placed at regular intervals along a wall, generally 16 inches center of one stud to the center of the next. To use this method, you start at a corner and measure along the wall in 16-inch lengths. But to start, you must take into account the thickness of the plaster and other factors. Therefore, the first stud from a major corner (where two outside walls meet) will be at 14-1/2 inches, and 16 inches thereafter for the second and subsequent studs. On interior walls (walls that do not form an outside wall) there will be two conditions, an inside corner and an outside corner. From an inside corner, measure in 16-3/4 inches to the first stud and 16 inches thereafter. From an outside corner, measure 17-1/2 inches to the first stud and 16 inches thereafter. To confirm that you have found the stud, you can do two things. The first is to look for

nails that hold the plasterboard to the wall. There will often be small marks. The second is to use a stud finder, a small inexpensive tool utilizing a free-moving magnetic needle which will move when it nears a nail. Move the stud finder along a vertical line where your measuring has determined that the stud is likely to be. If the magnet moves, you've found one. If it doesn't, try a run 1-1/2 inches on either side.

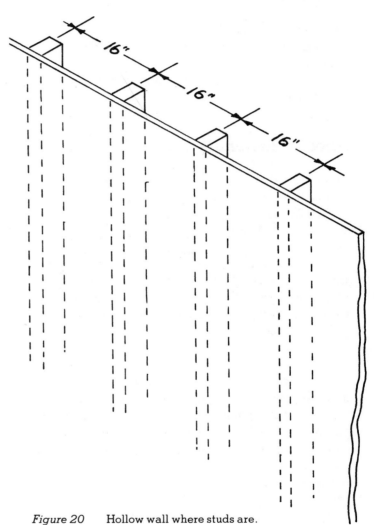

Figure 20   Hollow wall where studs are.

(2) The second method is the "rap" method. With the heel of your hand, rap along the wall. A hollow sound means no stud; a solid sound means you may have found one. The change in sound is subtle, but you can improve the odds by then using the stud finder as above, or using method three.

(3) Method three is like a fishing expedition. Using a small nail or a drill with a small bit, you make exploratory holes as inconspicuously as possible. This can be done right at the top of the baseboard or behind it if the baseboard can be easily removed. Or, if what you are putting up will cover part of the wall, the holes can be drilled in the area it will eventually cover. Use the measuring method to get an idea of where to start and drive the nail or drill the holes until you find a stud.

Once you find one stud, by what ever method or methods, the adjacent ones will be 16 inches on either side. But suppose finding or fastening to a stud or studs is impractical or impossible, what then? Glad you asked.

Special fasteners

The purpose of special fasteners is to get a grip in or behind a material—like plaster, drywall, plasterboard, or masonry—that won't or can't support the weight or stress with nails or screws.

For drywall or plaster, the Molly Fastener (a trademark of The Molly Co. for their expanding bolt) or an equivalent fastener will expand behind drywall or plaster to get a grip that is not likely to pull free. (See Fig. 21.)

To install these, drill a hole the size specified on the package the fastener came in. Slide the Molly bolt into the hole (the hole should be quite snug, so a *light* tap with a hammer may be needed to get the fastener seated firmly); then turn the screw clockwise. This pulls the sleeve up toward you and expands the wings behind the wall. Once the screw becomes tight (when the wings are fully extended) remove the screw, slide on the fixture or whatever you are hanging, and reinstall the screw. If you find that the screw is now too short to go through your fixture or wood, a longer one can be found at any hardware store. The screw can be removed and reinstalled as many times as is needed.

A toggle bolt or butterfly bolt works in a similar way. Its open wings hold behind the plaster or drywall.

A larger hole must be drilled for a toggle bolt than for a Molly, and the fixture *must* be put on the screw *before* the toggle is pushed through the hole. If the screw is removed after the butterfly is pushed through the wall, the wings will drop away down into the wall and a new one would be needed. The advantage of toggle bolts is that they can carry a slightly greater load than the Molly because of their larger wing area. (See Fig. 22.)

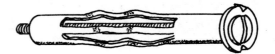

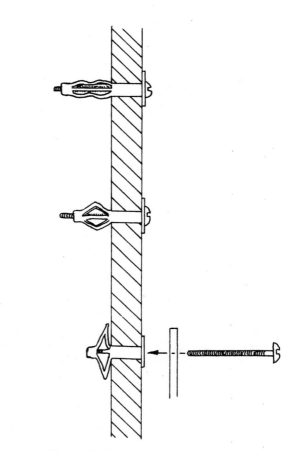

Figure 21   Using Molly bolts.

The third special fastener for plaster or drywall is the plastic anchor. It holds by applying pressure around the hole that it rests in. Because it has no wings behind the wall, it cannot hold as much weight as a Molly or a toggle. If you are in doubt about using a plastic anchor, use a Molly or a toggle. But if the weight or stress is light, a plastic an-chor is easier to use and the hole is easier to repair if you ever remove it. (See Fig. 23.)

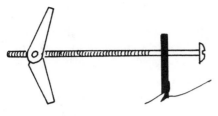

TOGGLE BOLT

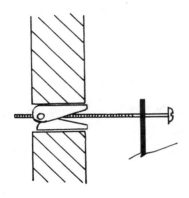

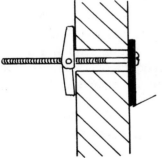

Figure 22

To install a plastic anchor, drill a hole the size specified on the package. Seat the anchor in the hole. If a tap with a hammer is needed, be sure it is gentle—too severe a rap can shatter the anchor. Push the screw through the fixture and drive the

Figure 23

PLASTIC ANCHOR

screw home. Again, longer screws are available if needed. The screws can be removed and replaced; but remember that each time this is done, the grip of the anchor is weakened.

For fastening into masonry and brick walls, there are three appropriate types of fasteners, all similar to plastic anchors in the way they work. They are raw plugs, lead anchors, and heavy-duty lead an-chors.

Raw plugs are small pieces of fiber material fitted into a hole drilled in the mortar between the blocks or bricks. Screws are driven into them. Lead an-chors are similar but for larger sizes (for No. 8 screws and up). Heavy- duty lead anchors require a much larger hole and accommodate lag bolts or machine bolts; they will handle much heavier weights and greater stresses.

Your hardware person will help you select the pro-per fastener and will help you with instructions for drilling the required holes and installing the fasteners.

Fasteners for ceilings

Like walls, ceilings have studs. Ceiling studs are called joists. Joists run across the ceiling at a right angle to the ridge (peak) of the roof and sit exactly on top of the wall studs. They can be found and receive attachments like wall studs, or special fasteners can be used. The same instructions as for the walls are used.

Planning and Design

Each project requires some planning and design. The design itself can be a large part of the satisfaction of a project you do yourself. I must confess a personal bias—I love to design and plan. I like to write a program, a step-by-step list of all the stages of a project from beginning to end, and check off each stage as I finish it. Try it!

Following you will find the factors I use. Add any others applicable to your project and remember that time spent in planning will save time in construction and often money spent for materials.

SURVEY

There are three basic elements to a survey: the past, the present and the future. The past consists of the ideas and hopes you've had, like, "I've always wanted a . . . in that corner," or, "Everytime I try to find that [blank] dictionary I . . ." or, "Whenever I try to get my bowling ball out of that closet I have to take out all the coats, tear the door off, and hire a bulldozer to put everything back." Collect as many of your past ideas together as you can.

The present has two aspects: what you want to store or display, and your considerations of aesthetics or appearance. The shelves must be able to store what you want to store now, and still not be so ugly that your house is condemned, your spouse divorces you, or your landlord evicts you.

The future is a little tricky. Consider any factors that will be changing—a new encyclopedia, moving soon, Uncle Fred is going to give me all those books, and so on. Adaptability is useful in a design. I know that it is difficult to foresee all the possibilities.

With survey in hand, I next apply the KISS system. KISS stands for, "Keep it simple, stupid." I say this to myself several times until I really am committed to keeping my project simple. My best designs have always been KISS designs. If I find myself with a design that is too complicated, I work it over until I find a way to make it simpler, more straightforward, easier to build. A little extra time spent at this stage will (or can) save hours later when you find that you have "painted yourself into a corner."

Display vs. storage

The difference between shelves for display and shelves exclusively for storage is the design and the quality of materials, plus the intention of the builder.

A simple, rugged design made of construction-grade wood will serve very well for storage shelves in a garage or basement. The same materials with a different design could make a beautiful set of shelves in a den or family room. Conversely, the most utilitarian design can be used in a decorative way also. So the distinction of display vs. storage is really one of intent rather than execution.

Movable or fixed shelves

There are two considerations here: being able to move the entire unit, and being able to move the individual shelves in the unit. Units with movable components or movable units are more difficult to build, but they can adjust to accommodate the changes in your life.

Weights and loads

The amount of weight on a shelf is its *load*. The load you intend for a shelf will to some degree determine what material and thickness you will need. As a general rule of thumb, I have found that

5/8-inch or 3/4-inch material is suitable for all kinds of indoor shelves, providing the spans (the distance between supports) are kept to less than four feet. Obviously, if you plan to store auto batteries or bags of cement, a thicker shelf material is required, e.g., 2 × 10's or 2 × 12's.

If you are uncertain whether the material you are selecting can handle the weight you want, test out a piece by placing it between two supports (like two chairs or two piles of lumber at the yard), put some weight on it, and see how it responds.

How big?

Now there is a good question. The easiest way I have found for figuring out how large shelves need to be is to lay out the materials I wish to store or display and measure. I will occasionally eliminate a piece or two that appears too large.

Next, make a sketch and write the dimensions on it. Try, if possible, to apply the measurements to the actual location of the shelves to get a feel for how they will look.

You can also check with your local furniture stores if you are planning a decorative shelf system. Bring a tape measure and actually measure and write down the dimensions of pieces if they seem to be the right size.

LIGHTING

In designing decorative shelving systems, consider lighting. It can add dramatic effects and beauty to your system. Lighting can come from many sources and need not be elaborate or expensive to be effective. For example, a standing lamp near the shelves can throw a pleasant light and cast lovely shadows. So consider how you can place existing floor, table, or hanging lamps.

A second light source would be from the ceiling. Fixtures recessed into the ceiling, or track lights (where an electrical track is fastened to the ceiling and swivel-lights are plugged into it), are two options for getting light from the ceiling. These require some installation savvy, but any good lighting dealer will be glad to help you work out the details.

TIP A useful tip: A shelf can be made more sag-resistant (and a decorative touch gained at the same time) by fastening strips of wood or metal along the edges of the shelf. The strips can be 1 × 2 wood, smaller pieces of hardwood, aluminium strips or angles, etc.

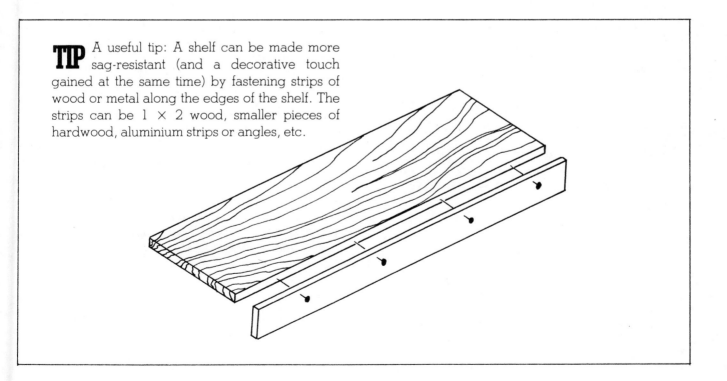

Ceiling light can also be created by bouncing light off the ceiling. This is done by aiming a light source from a table or the floor toward the ceiling so that the light will reflect down onto the shelves. This can also be done with existing lamps.

Another option for lighting is to install fixtures under the shelves. There is a wide variety of special fixtures made just for this purpose. A lighting dealer usually stocks a few of these, and a look through some of his catalogues will often reveal others. Sometimes available fixtures may require a little modification, so ask the dealer for advice.

Consider the possibility of making your own under-shelf lighting. You will have two types to choose from.

The first is fluorescent, the long thin tubes. There is a wide variety of lengths to choose from, and the bulbs themselves are available in a wide variety of different tints: "cool white" is very white and bright; "day light" is slightly pink in tone and softer; "pink" is a much pinker light and quite soft; Gro-Lite® or the equivalent gives a purplish light that stimulates plant growth. Fluorescent lights give off very little heat, but do produce a lot of ultra-violet light. If you plan to display valuable art objects or old books, keep in mind that the ultra-violet can fade colors and cause some deterioration of old papers and canvas.

The second type is incandescent (regular light bulb type). A special type of long, thin incandescent bulbs, called showcase bulbs, is available for under-shelf applications. Incandescents produce a more yellow light than fluorescents and tend to cast harsher shadows. They do produce considerable heat but very little ultra-violet.

In making your own lighting, disguising the fixtures will add a finished look. A piece of 1 × 3 nailed or screwed along the front edge of the shelf extending below it will hide the fixture. Or, a piece of opaque Plexiglas bent into an "L" (you can have this done by your Plexiglas dealer) and installed upside-down under the shelf will also hide the fixtures. (See Fig. 25.)

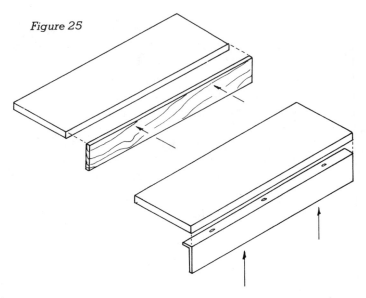

Figure 25

FINISHES

Unfinished wood accumulates dust and dirt in the pores and grain of the wood. After a while the wood will be discolored unevenly and will begin to look shabby. A finish applied to the wood will prevent this, and can really add to the beauty and durability of your project.

There are a variety of finishes that can be used for wood shelves. For simplicity, I'll divide them into three types: paints, clear finishes, and my special favorite (which I'll save for last).

Paints are available in two types: water-based, or latex; and oil-based, usually called enamel. Both are applied using a spray, roller, or brush. The differences are that oil can cover a greater area per quart (or gallon) and will create a more durable surface than water-based paints. Water-based paints, on the other hand, dry much faster (usually at least twice as fast as oil); for latex, moreover, painting tools can be cleaned with warm water and soap, whereas tools used for oil-based paints must be cleaned in turpentine or paint thinner. Water-based or latex paints have improved a great deal over the past five years and new advances are being made all the time. I recommend them because I hate to clean brushes in turpentine.

Paints come in three glosses or sheens: flat (no

gloss at all), semi-gloss (soft gloss like the cover of a magazine), and gloss (very shiny like a clean pane of glass). Gloss and semi-gloss are best for shelves since they make a smooth surface that can be washed.

Read the manufacturer's directions for application before you buy any finish. I have found the directions to be excellent almost without exception. (The only times that I have gotten into trouble with a paint or finish are when I have disregarded some or all of the directions or tried to use the finish for something it was never intended.) A glance through the directions beforehand will give you an idea of what you are getting into. If the process seems too involved for you, check with your hardware or paint store person; often there are alternatives that will give almost the same result in fewer steps.

Clear finishes include shellac, varnish, and polyurethane. All of these finishes coat the surface and each has advantages and disadvantages. I'll cover each of them briefly here; but for complete information, talk to your hardware or paint store person, or check into a good book on finishing.

Shellac forms a hard surface and dries quickly. It has a slight darkening effect on wood. Its disadvantage is that it is not resistant to water, detergents, or alcohol, and is therefore less durable.

Varnish also forms a hard surface, but is quite slow to dry and can be difficult to apply. It adds a slight yellow or amber tint to the wood. Varnish must be sanded between coats, but is resistant to water, alcohol, and detergents.

Polyurethane is the most durable of all the finishes mentioned so far. It dries faster than varnish and is easier to apply. It enhances the grain of wood and adds a slight amber tint. A difficulty I have found with polyurethane is that mineral spirits are required to clean brushes, and I have had a very hard time getting brushes clean at all. There is a new type of polyurethane on the market that you wipe on with a clean, lint-free cloth. This would seem to be ideal—when you are done, you throw the rag away. But since I have not tried it, talk to your dealer and get another opinion.

Under a clear finish you may want to color the wood with a *stain*. However, a stain is not a finish. Wood which has only been stained and not finished further has the same liability as wood with no finish at all. There are two types of stain I recommend.

The first is oil stain. Rather than coat the wood, this type of stain soaks into the wood and is available in a wide variety of colors. It is applied with a rag or very fine steel wool and will give an even tone easily. But it is a one-shot deal, that is, the color you get when you first apply it is pretty much what you will end up with.

The second type, and my preference, is pigmented wiping stain. It is darker and more opaque than oil stains, and so can be used to hide the grain of the wood or make it look like another wood. But it can also be applied more lightly just to enhance the grain. Since this stain can be used in several coats, go too light with the first coat if you can; you can easily make it darker, but the reverse is not true. Wiping stain is the easiest for the do-it-yourselfer since it is more "forgiving" than oil.

Now, my personal *favorite* of the finishes—*tung oil*. Tung oil is chemically similar to the natural oils in wood and will beautify the grain while providing a protective coating that resists water, alcohol, detergents (God forbid you should ever use soap and water on furniture), etc. Tung oil is applied with your hand or with a piece of cotton cloth—no clean-up problems. Gloss is determined by how many coats you apply, the more-the glossier. Homer Formby markets tung oil and other products for wood care and finishes and I highly recommend them. You won't be disappointed.

* * *

One last word about design and planning: Originality. In spite of what your third-grade art teacher might have told you, originality is not required. Ideas are abundant and you'll see great ones all over the place, and I hope in this book. Apply the ideas to your projects. Don't misunderstand—use your own ideas by all means, but don't feel bad using those of others as well.

Part Two
Prefabricated Parts

Shelf Brackets and Angle Irons

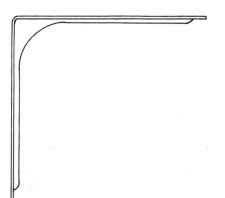

Figure 26 ANGLE IRON

SHELF BRACKETS

A common hardware and building supply item, shelf brackets and angle irons are a quick and easy way to attach shelves.

The difference between shelf brackets and angle irons is that shelf brackets are designed and manufactured specifically for holding up shelves, and therefore have some extra bracing, or gussetting. Angle irons are simply steel bars bent at a right angle that have no gussetting or diagonal support. (See Fig. 26.)

Using shelf brackets will often give a better result because the gussetting will help to make the shelf's

surface steady. With angle irons, the shelf surface can be a little "springy," particularly if the weight on it is great.

But do not disgard angle irons altogether as they have useful applications. Because of the absence of gussetts, they can be used inverted. This will help to hide the bracket. (See Fig. 27.)

In putting up shelves with angle irons or shelf brackets, attaching them firmly to the wall or uprights is crucial. The sections on "how to find a stud" (p. 25) and "special fasteners" (p. 26) offer some tips you can use.

Figure 27
Inverted angle iron.

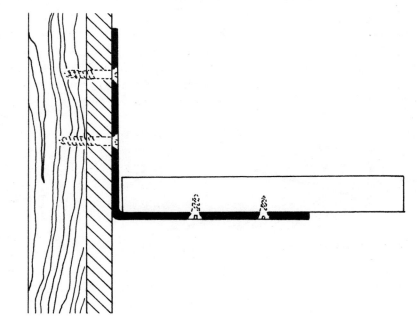

Planning with shelf brackets is easy and design possibilities are limitless. The brackets come usually for 6-inch, 8-inch, 10-inch, and 12-inch shelf widths. Attaching shelves to brackets is done usually by drilling pilot holes and driving wood screws. Of course, the shelves can be allowed to simply rest on the brackets without being fastened, but this is usually not safe.

Pre-cut and pre-finished shelves can be used with your brackets, if you wish, and can be found in hardware and do-it-yourself stores in widths of 8, 10, and 12 inches, and in lengths of 2, 2-1/2, 3, 4, and 6 feet.

One word of caution in using pre-finished shelves: if the shelves are laminated (covered with Formica), driving screws through them can shatter the laminate. Use the foam tape for these.

Shelf hangers

There is another bracket which could be best called a hanger. These brackets are metal, bent as shown and hooked together to form tiers of hanging shelves. (See Fig. 28.)

The only trick in installing these is to get a firm grip in the ceiling with the screw eyes that hold the shelves up. Be sure to use screw eyes that are long enough to go all the way through the plaster and into the rafters or studs behind.

These hangers are generally used in utility applications. Thick wood like 2 × 10's or 2 × 12's is often used for the shelves. Check the package of the hangers for weight limitations.

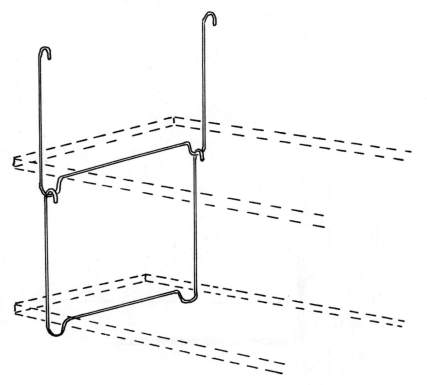

Figure 28   Shelf hangers.

Prefabricated Units

A glance through the catalogue of any large chain store (Sears, Montgomery Ward, etc.) will show many different types and sizes of prefabricated shelves that "any eight-year-old" can put together. These units are most often made of two materials, steel and plastic.

Steel shelves arrive in "instant powdered form" in a box with (hopefully) all the materials and hardware needed to assemble them.

The designs and assembly instructions from manufacturer to manufacturer vary greatly, so I can only offer some general tips to help you in putting one of these together. The first is to keep an eye on the metal edges—they can be brutally sharp. A pair of work gloves can be very useful in protecting your hands; and if you don't want the floor you are working on to be marred or scratched, a blanket or a piece of carpet should be used to protect it. Another general tip: I have found that to assemble these units with the nuts and bolts *finger-tight*—as tight as you can get them with your fingers—allows you to move the parts around enough to make them line up much more easily. Once the unit is assembled finger-tight, you can then stand it up, make it straight and square, and then proceed to tighten all the nuts and bolts with tools.

The plastic units are usually found in the furniture department already assembled. All you need to do with these units is to stack them together. Do not select these for storing gold bullion, auto batteries, or other objects heavier than books.

Furniture stores sell "wall systems" or "wall units" in many styles and price ranges. These are decorative, strong, and can be moved when you do. They can be somewhat difficult to assemble; the dealer will often provide helpful advice. These units or systems have many accessories, such as cabinets, wine racks, bars, desks, lighting, etc. Check with the various dealers in your area and

you will find a lot of them. One word of warning: do not buy one of these just from a photo in a catalogue. Although the camera never lies, it doesn't always tell the truth. A photo won't tell you how well the pieces fit together, whether the drawers (if any) slide smoothly, and so on. Insist on seeing a unit assembled. It is often a good idea to ask to speak to the person who assembled the unit for the store. He or she can often alert you to a problem you could solve in advance or a factor you might have overlooked in ordering (like, is my floor level?).

TIP Another hint: Look for these units at unfinished-furniture stores. They often carry the same brands as the fancy stores and sell them at lower prices. You might also find an unfinished substitute at a much lower price.

Speaking of unfinished-furniture stores, they can be a fruitful source of shelving. They have many different sizes and styles. Almost all of their offerings will come pre-assembled. Tips on finishing can be found in the "Planning and Design" section (pp. 30–31.)

Another use of unfinished-furniture stores, or of any furniture store for that matter, is as a source of ideas. They will have catalogues galore that you will be able to see with a little prodding. Those ideas combined with the construction techniques given in this book should yield pleasing results.

It goes without saying that the more of the work you do yourself, the lower your cost will be. Therefore, the opposite is true as well. Hopefully you will find the balance that is best for you.

Standards and Supports

First, let's define our terms. A *standard* is a piece of metal or wood that, when attached to a solid surface, will hold a number of shelf supports. Standards come in a lot of different types and lengths.

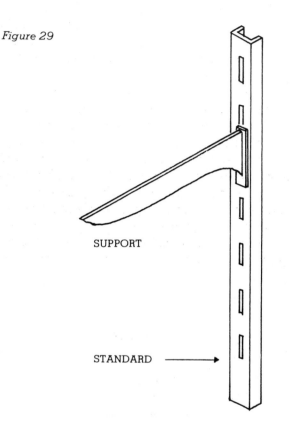

Figure 29

SUPPORT

STANDARD ⟶

A *support* is a wood or metal bracket that attaches to a standard; it is the part that the shelf actually rests on.

Standards and supports are generally sold in systems, and parts of one system are usually not interchangeable with parts of another. Therefore, in planning a unit of standards and supports, try to buy all the hardware at one time. If the dealer does not have enough materials to complete the job, do a little shopping around first to see if more components made by the same manufacturer are available, or if another dealer has enough to accommodate your needs.

INSTALLING A STANDARD-AND-SUPPORT SYSTEM

Several manufacturers sell the shelves already cut and finished. Sizes vary somewhat from manufacturer to manufacturer, but lengths generally run 18 inches, 24 inches, 36 inches, 48 inches, and 60 inches. Widths are 8 inches, 10 inches, and 12 inches. Of course, it is not necessary to buy the premade shelves that go with the system. You can easily make your own from plywood, shelving pine, particle board, hardwood, etc. Since most of the premade shelves are 5/8 inch or 3/4 inch thick, the maximum span between supports should not be more than 4 feet. You can mix the length of shelves, if you like, but follow that guideline.

Installing the system is easy, providing that you have a *stable starting point.* A plumb bob (a long string with a weight on one end) and a level are useful tools for getting a starting point. Our goal is to get the shelves straight and level and the standards straight up and down. However, since houses are seldom exactly square or level, some adjusting will almost always be needed.

In finding the starting point and installing the shelves, I strongly recommend that you first lay the pieces out on the floor to test the arrangement you are building. Transferring the individual parts to the wall is then done in an organized way and keeps confusion to a minimum. Keep in mind that the shelves should extend past the supports by at least 2 inches so they will stay on the supports and not tip.

Our stable starting point will be our first standard. Transfer its location from the floor to the wall; holding it in place, make a pencil mark on the wall through the top screw hole. If you are mounting to the studs, the screws usually provided will be fine;

if you are using Molly bolts or plastic anchors, you will drill at this mark and install the fastener.

Without tightening the screw, install the support so that it can swing freely. Stand back and see if it is vertical. If you are uncertain, check it with the plumb bob by holding the unweighted end of the string near the top of the support and letting the weight swing freely. The string will hang exactly vertical. See that the standard is parallel to the string.

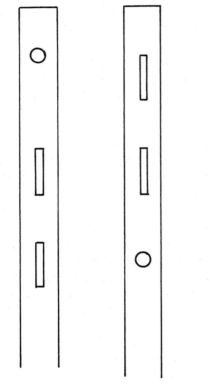

Figure 30
Note the different positions of the round screw holes.

Once the first standard is vertical, mark the remaining screw holes and complete its installation by putting in the other screws (or Molly bolts or plastics anchors) and tighten them all in place. This first standard will become the stable starting point.

The next step is to install the remaining standards. Check each to see that it is oriented the same, top-to-bottom, as the others—I have found that occasionally the distance of the first screw hole from the

end of a standard may not be the same at both ends. I know that this might sound a little confusing, but one look will quickly show you what I am talking about. (See Fig. 30.)

Measure the distance left to right that the second support will be from the first. Measure the distance from the ceiling to the first standard and transfer this distance to the second. Now you should know where the next standard goes. Install the top screw as before. Make sure that it is vertical as you did with the first; then install the remaining screws. Continue in this way until all of the standards are in place.

> **TIP** If you are using standards of different lengths, establish a stable starting point as above. Next, install a shelf bracket and then, using a shelf, the next standard, and another bracket, hold up a shelf and all the supporting hardware. Get someone to help you by putting a level on the shelf and adjust the second standard up or down until the shelf is level. Then pencil mark the top hole in the second standard, drive in its screws, and proceed with the others in the same way.

When installing the supports on the standards, make sure that they are firmly seated. If the support seems to wobble from left to right it is most likely not properly seated. If the support will not seat itself with a few taps of your palm, protect the support with a block of wood and tap it *gently* in place with a hammer. (Caution: Occasionlly one of the screws that fastens the standards to the wall will prevent the support from seating properly, so check this before you get too energetic with the hammer. If this is the case, usually one screw can be removed without seriously weakening the hold to the wall.)

Once the supports are in place, slide on the shelves and . . . *Voilà!*

Variations

A variety of the standard-and-support system uses narrow tracks of metal with small clips. These hold the shelves up between uprights by supporting the ends of the shelves. (See Fig. 31.) Four clips are needed for each shelf, along with four of the tracks along the uprights. These are often installed in cabinets or where there are two opposing walls less than 4 feet apart. Their advantage is that they are not very visible and are often less expensive than the "standard" standard-and-support systems.

Another variety of the standard-and-support system consists of special wall paneling that has the standards built into it and special supports that fit the standards. This makes the shelf hardware all but invisible. You install this system according to the directions supplied, but basically it is installed just like any other paneling—though with greater care to anchoring it, since it will have to carry weight. The great advantage of this system (marketed under the trademark of Royal System and other names) is that you get paneling and shelving all in one step.

Systems like the Royal System have many accessories, like hanging cabinets, desks, special lighting, etc. These can sometimes be adapted to other hardware and can be a great source of ideas for additions to your own design or plan.

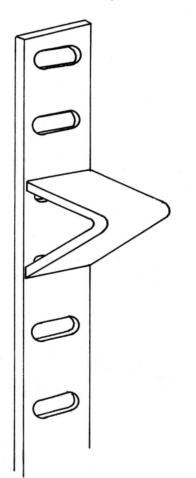

Figure 31

Spindle System

The spindle system of prefabricated shelving has become very popular in recent years because of its great versatility, ease of assembly, and variety of styles. The system is available either finished or unfinished.

Let's define the terms we'll be using in describing this system.

A *spindle* is the upright of the system. It is a turned or carved piece of wood with a threaded recess on each end. *Connectors* are small threaded dowels that screw into the recesses in the spindles through the holes in the shelves.

The *shelves* have holes that are sized to allow the connectors to fit through so that they can be screwed into the spindles. Where two shelves are fastened together over one spindle, the ends of the shelves are lapped. Therefore, in planning your purchase, list the single-lapped, double-lapped and straight shelves separately. (See Fig. 33.)

A *finial* is a connector on one end and a finished trim piece on the other. They are used at the top of the shelves, or at the bottom as feet, or both.

Shelf spacers are used when you would like to join two spindles together with no shelf in between. The

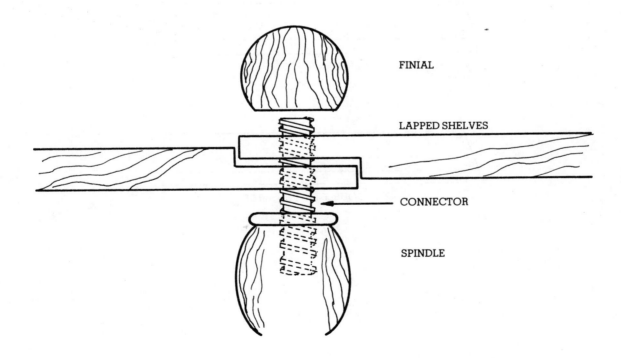

FINIAL

LAPPED SHELVES

CONNECTOR

SPINDLE

Figure 32

spacer takes the space that the shelf would have taken.

After you have created your design, a materials list is a must. Total the number of spindles, connectors, shelves (straight, lapped on one edge, lapped on both edges), finials, and spacers you will need.

With your materials list in hand, head for a good hardware store, a do-it-yourself store, or a lumberyard to find the parts. Try to find parts that are all from one manufacturer. Although the parts may look interchangeable, there are often minor differences in size and style.

Assembly of spindle shelves is simple. Start from the bottom and work toward the top. Two materials to have on hand during assembly are a piece of fine sandpaper and a can of silicone spray lubricant. Soap can be used if you don't have the spray. The silicone spray or soap is used to encourage reluctant parts.

Figure 33

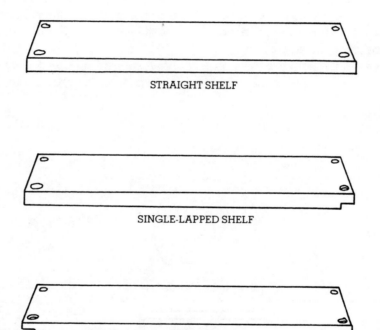

STRAIGHT SHELF

SINGLE-LAPPED SHELF

DOUBLE-LAPPED SHELF

Part Three
Build It Yourself

Stacking Shelves

The illustration shows a very simple way to hold up shelves using a pile of bricks or blocks. To construct a shelf system like this, just get some ordinary bricks (lumberyard stock), stack them as high as you like, make as many shelves as you like. Keep in mind the load restrictions of the material you select, as sag in the shelves is always a factor.

Keep in mind that the main drawback of this system is sway from side to side. Four or five layers is a safe limit as to height.

This kind of shelf, although very simple, can be quite attractive. You can use almost anything for the "bricks," like wooden packing crates (open side facing front), milk crates (wire or plastic), concrete blocks (the decorative ones are nice), even books!

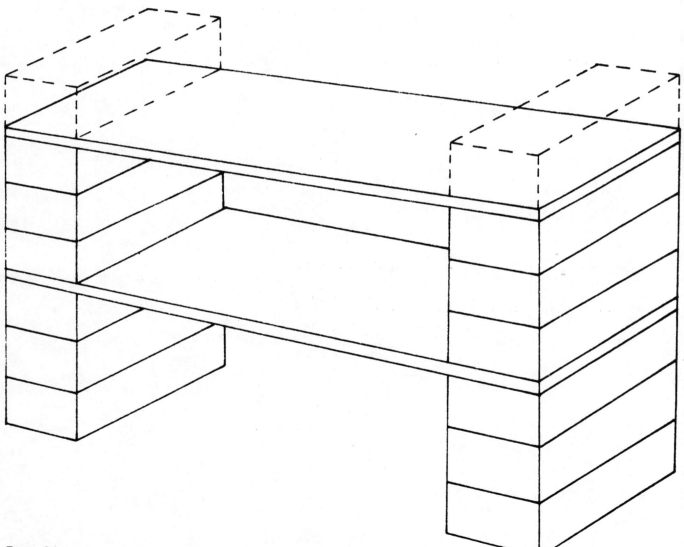

Figure 34

Hanging Shelves

Another method of building shelves is to hang them from the ceiling or walls. We will look into two ways here.

Figure 35

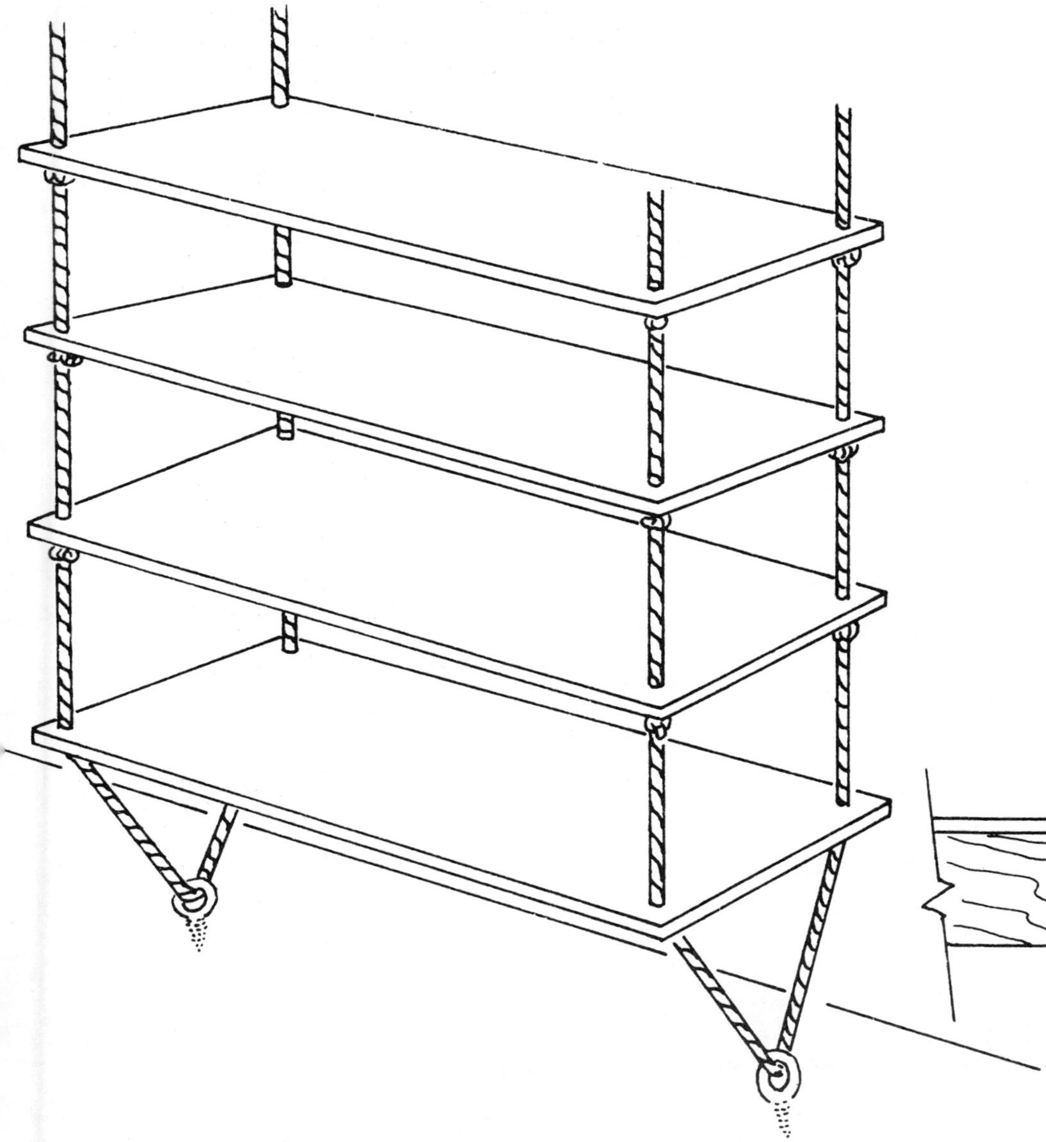

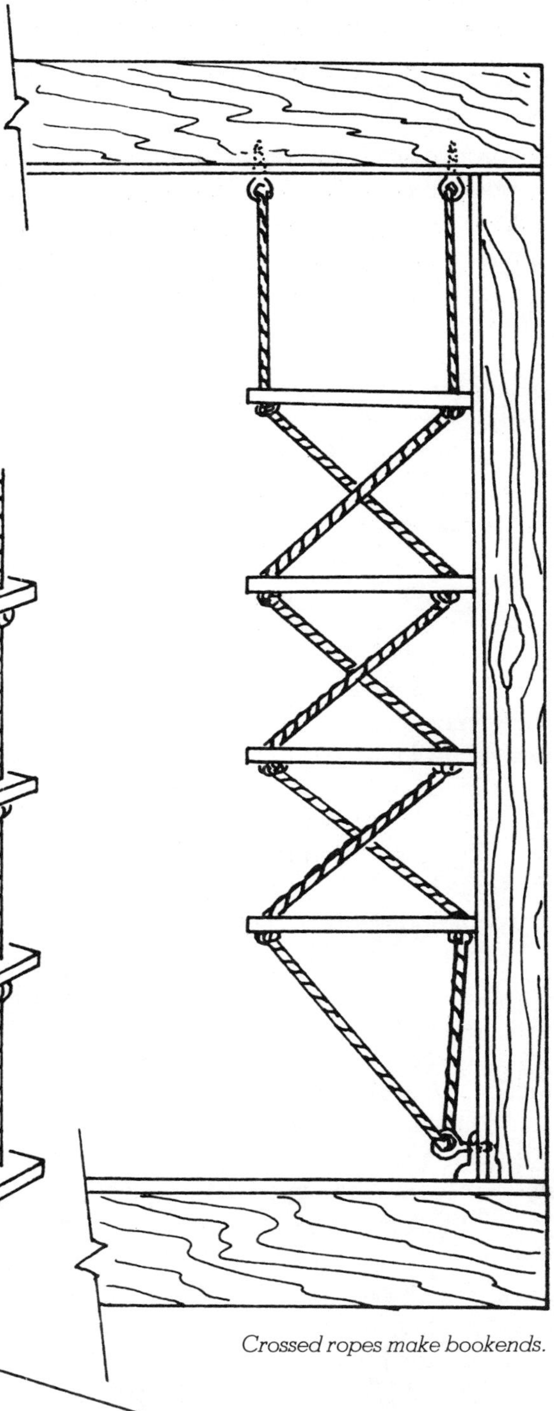

Crossed ropes make bookends.

ROPE-HANGING SHELVES

Screw eyes properly anchored in the ceiling or wall and ordinary hemp rope or clothesline with a few pieces of wood or Plexiglas will produce attractive and functional shelves at low cost. This method of construction is quite simple and has the added advantage of being usable in awkward places like in front of a window (for plants), or in the middle of a room as a divider (without blocking the view), and so on.

The only disadvantage of this system that I know of is sway, so if you use these in an area where the shelves are likely to be knocked a bit, be sure to anchor them down (as shown in Fig. 35). This will not totally eliminate sway, but will reduce it dramatically. If your shelves will be less vulnerable, bottom anchoring may not be needed at all.

The first step in building this system is design. Determine how large the shelves will be and approximately how much weight they will carry. Almost any kind of wood can be used, but I recommend that it not be thinner than 1/2 inch. I prefer 3/4 inch or thicker. You can use plywood, particle (or composition) board, or solid woods like pine. Ten- or twelve-inch pine shelving stock works well. If you choose Plexiglas, be sure to consider the edge-bending technique (p. 19) to improve strength and decrease sag.

For rope, my preference is hemp (or manilla), although nylon, Dacron, polypropylene, clothesline, and others can be used. My experience with synthetics is that they tend to stretch more than hemp, and sometimes stretch unevenly if the load on the shelf is not balanced. But check with your hardware person. New types of rope are being introduced all the time and one of them could be dandy.

The following is a rough guideline for selecting rope size for hemp: for weight up to 100 pounds (including shelves) use 1/4-inch rope; for 100-to-200 pounds use 3/8-inch rope; for 200-to-300 pounds use 1/2-inch rope. Nylon or Dacron can be one size smaller, i.e., 1/4 inch for up to 200 pounds, 3/8 inch for 200 pounds or over. These

figures are very conservative and well within the tensile strength rates of the ropes.

Screw-eye sizes should be: 1 inch for use with 1/4-inch rope; 1-1/4 inch for use with 3/8-inch rope; and 1-1/2 inch for 1/2-inch rope. You may have to use a larger size if there is any doubt that the screw portion will reach a stud or other solid support. The whole system is dependent on the firmness of the screw eyes, so take a little extra care in selecting and mounting them.

If you choose wood for your shelves, determine the sizes before you go to the lumberyard. Ask the dealer to cut the wood to size if you have any doubts about your ability to handle the cutting. There may be a small charge to do so, but the final result will be worth the little extra money.

Now to the actual building. The knot system is shown in Figure 35. If you have chosen this system, you will have to drill holes in the shelves for the ropes to pass through. It is a good idea to drill all the shelves at one time so they will line up exactly. To do this, either clamp or tie the boards or plexi pieces in a stack. Put a piece of scrap under the stack to protect the surface you are drilling on. Make a mark at each corner (and in the center if you are using a center support) approximately 1/2-inch from each edge.

Figure 36

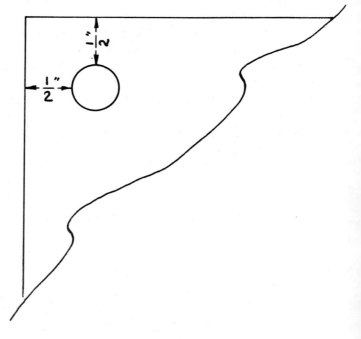

44

Square the sides together so that each board is exactly on top of the one(s) below and drill straight down through all of the boards at one time. Use a drill bit exactly the same size as the rope you are using. Hold the stack tightly as you drill to prevent the boards from sliding around. The hole will be slightly snug so that the knots that support the shelves will not have to be large.

Next, mount the screw eyes in the ceiling or wall. The bottom anchors, if you will be using them, should be left for last so that they can be precisely positioned. See the section "How to Find a Stud" (p. 25) for the easiest method of stud finding.

The next step will be to cut the rope. If you are using the straight-hanging method and are anchoring to the floor, make each piece of rope about four feet longer than the distance from the floor to the ceiling. If you will be criss-crossing the ropes as shown in Figure 35, make the ropes about twice as long as the length from floor to ceiling. If your shelves will be free-hanging, make the ropes about two feet longer than the total height of the shelves plus the distance from the top shelf to the screw eyes. This rough method to determine the length

will waste some rope, but it is much easier to cut it a little shorter when the job is done than it is to cut it a little longer somewhere in the middle. (See Fig. 37.)

Getting the shelf-supporting knots in the right place can be the most difficult part of the job. Here is the method that I have used with success. (1) Lay the ropes out on the floor or table with the ends together stretched out straight. (2) Determine how far off the floor the first shelf will be. For the straight-hanging or criss-cross method add two feet to this distance, measure the total on the rope, and mark the spot with a felt-tipped pen. (If your shelves will be free-hanging with no floor anchor, skip this step as no extra length is needed.) (3) Determine the distance between the lowest and next higher shelf. If you are using the straight-hanging method, add two inches to this distance for the knot and mark on the rope as before. If you are using the criss-cross method, actually lay it out as it will be, measure the length of rope, add two inches, and mark. (4) Continue until you have made the marks for every shelf. (5) Tie the lowest knot on each of the four (or six) ropes, leaving the marker line just above the knot. The shelf will hide

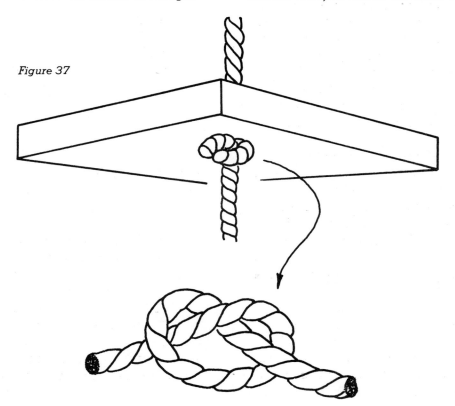

Figure 37

the line. (6) Slide the lowest shelf onto the ropes so that the knots are below the shelf. (7) Tie the next higher set of knots, slide the shelf on, and so on until all the shelves are on the ropes.

To put the shelves up, pick up the whole assembled stack and rest them on top of your ladder. Tie the ropes to the screw eyes as shown in Figure 38 and let the shelves hang. Major adjustments can be made by retying the knots at the screw eyes; minor adjustments are made at each supporting knot by pushing the shelf up a little and working the knot up or down as required.

Install the lower anchors if you are using them, fasten and trim off any excess rope, and that's it.

The shelves, if you use wood, can be finished either before or after installation. Plexiglas shelves should be polished before installing.

Figure 38

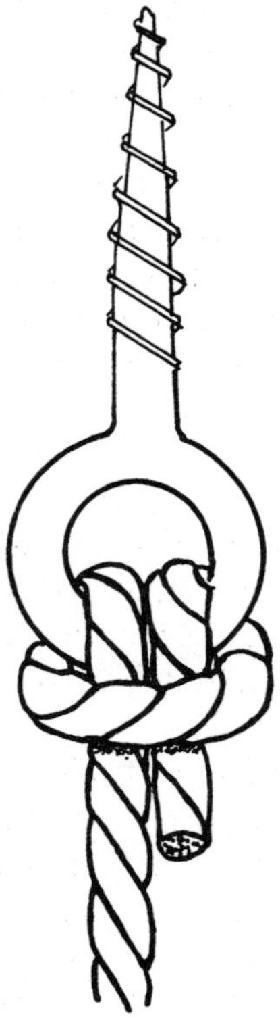

CHAIN-HANGING SHELVES

The same type of shelf system can be constructed using chain. Chain has the advantage of minimal stretch and great strength. In addition, many chain types can be quite decorative and shelf positions can be more easily changed if that is a requirement.

The preparation of the shelves themselves is the same as for rope-hanging shelves. The size of the holes should be adjusted to be as close as possible to the size of the chain. The chain is attached to the screw eyes using "S" hooks.

The biggest difference between the rope and chain methods is that making knots in chain is not practical. Here are two methods for holding the shelves up.

The first method uses nuts, bolts, and washers. Use bolts about one inch longer than the diameter of the hole you drilled for the chain in the shelf. Each bolt will need two nuts and two washers. If you are using a decorative chain with large openings, fender washers (large washers with small holes) can be used with 3/16-inch or 1/4-inch bolts, a size that is generally usable for most sizes of chain. The assembly technique is shown in Figure 39: (1) Run a nut up toward the head of the bolt; (2) slide on one washer; (3) slide bolt through the chain at the desired height; (4) slide on one washer; (5) run on the second nut; (6) center the assemblage so that the length of bolt is about the same on either side of the chain. The shelves can later be moved by simply moving the bolt assemblies.

The second method is to make small pieces of solid wood that fit snugly into the chain openings. Simply wedge each piece into each of the four (or six) chains at the height you want the shelf. The wood block should fit tightly enough in the openings that they do not fall out, but should be free enough to make changing them simple. The weight of the shelf and what is on it will prevent them from getting too loose. I recommend making the blocks a little larger than needed and trimming them down with a knife.

The chain system is useful if you would want to change the height of the shelves very often. Either system can be moved easily.

The units are assembled in the same way as the rope units. With chain, however, you have the alternative of putting the chains up first and sliding the shelves up from bottom to top.

Figure 39

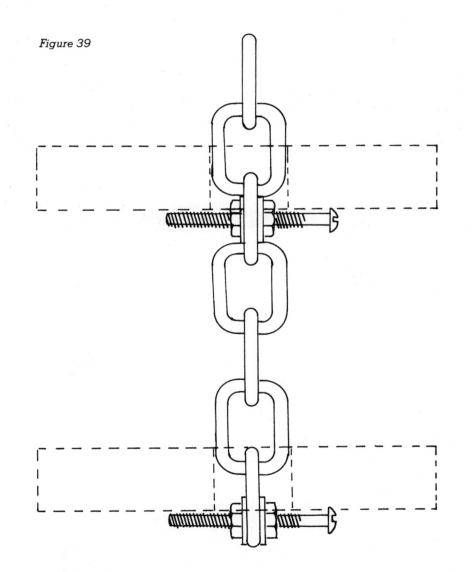

Threaded-Rod System

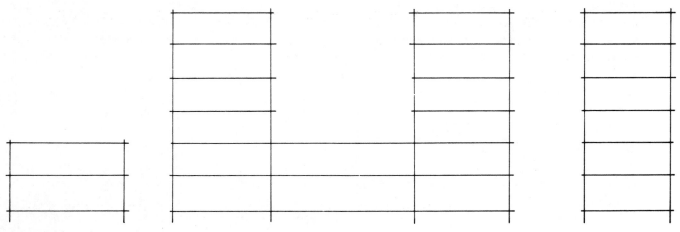

Figure 40

Threaded rod is like a very long bolt with no heads. It comes in standard sizes: 1/4-inch diameter, 3/8-inch diameter, and 1/2-inch diameter. Smaller sizes than 1/4 inch are generally not usable as they bend too easily. Appearance rather than strength would be the determining factor in the selection of the diameter you will use, since the 1/4-inch diameter is generally strong enough for all but the most rugged applications.

The most commonly available length of threaded rod is 3 feet. You will find the three-footers at most hardware stores and lumberyards. If, however, you want your shelf system to be taller than 3 feet, you can sometimes find 6-foot lengths or have them ordered for you. Another option you have is to join two (or more) three- footers together using a special adapter that is readily available. (See Fig. 41.)

In buying the rod, I suggest that you buy zinc-plated (also known as galvanized) rods, nuts, and washers. The plating prevents rust, making this system usable both indoors and outdoors.

This type of shelf system is very easily built, very versatile, and simple to change. By dressing it up, it can be a pleasant addition to a living room or study, a handsome room divider, etc. By using

thicker rod and wood, you can use it in a garage for storing heavy objects, in a greenhouse, tool shed—you name it.

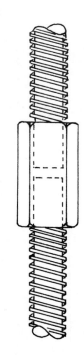

Figure 41

Adapter to hold together two lengths of threaded rod.

As shown in Figure 40, you can build almost any arrangement with this system. You can vary the width as well as the length of the shelves, move them whenever you want to. For the shelves themselves, you can use 3/4-inch plywood, pine shelving, or particle (composition) board. Plexiglas or hardwood can be used for more decorative applications.

In building these shelves, the design is first. Make a rough sketch and write in the dimensions you will use. Next, make a materials list. List the rods, shelves, and so on. You will need two nuts and two washers at each point where the rods go through the shelf, one nut and washer below and one nut and washer above. The reason for this is to give the unit more strength and prevent racking. You can also add "crutch tips" to the bottom and top of the rods to prevent marring the floor or just for appearance. A crutch tip is the little rubber cap you see on the foot of crutches. They are available in most hardware stores in sizes that match the rod, and they come in white and black.

You can get the wood or plexi shelves cut to size by your dealer or cut them yourself. Once you have your materials together, drilling the shelves is next. The drill size should be the size just larger

than the size of the rod: 5/16 inch for 1/4-inch rod; 7/16 inch for 3/8-inch rod; 9/16 inch for 1/2-inch rod. This will make the shelves easy to slide into place as you assemble.

To drill, take all the shelves that will be in the same vertical column, put them in a stack, square them together, and drill all at the same time. Put a scrap block of wood under the stack to protect the surface you are drilling on. Make sure you drill straight down, not at an angle. You must leave enough wood between the edge of the shelf and the hole when you drill. A rough guideline would be: leave 1/2 inch minimum from each edge for 1/4-inch or 3/8-inch rod; leave 3/4 inch from each edge for 1/2-inch rod. You can leave more if you desire and the overhang can be quite attractive.

Once all the shelves are drilled, check the fit. Start your assembly from the bottom and work up to the top. Put the nuts on "finger-tight" until the whole system is loosely assembled. Then, using a level or by eye, adjust each shelf until it is in the position you want. The nuts can now be snugged up using a wrench, tight enough to be firm, but not so tight as to damage the wood or crack the Plexiglas.

After the system is assembled, the unit can be painted if you wish. Use a paint for metal such as Rustoleum® or the like. But if you paint, you do limit your ability to change the shelves around, because as you move the nuts they will plow the paint out of the threads on the rods. An alternative is to slip pieces of tubing over the rods as you assemble. A check with your hardware dealer or plumbing supply company will reveal several types you can use. Also, most Plexiglas dealers carry several sizes and colors of plexi tubing that could be used as well. They are available in a variety of colors, the most common being black, white, and clear.

Personally, I like the appearance of the system with the rods left plain and the shelves stained dark.

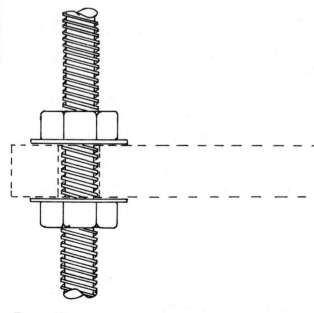

Figure 42

Pipe System

Pipe has been used for shelf supports for a long time. A fairly recent innovation, PVC (polyvinyl chloride) or plastic pipe has made using piping a lot easier and well within the reach of the mythical "average do-it-yourselfer." Plastic pipe is worked with ordinary hand tools like a saw, file, etc., and doesn't require threading because the pieces are assembled with a solvent glue. The designs shown in Figures 44 and 45 were put together for use with plastic pipe, but will work just as well with metal—if you are a plumber or have a plumbing supply person with the patience of Job.

PVC pipe is available in a variety of diameters: 1/2 inch, 3/4 inch, 1 inch, 1-1/4 inch, 1-1/2 inch, 2 inch, and so on. One inch is a useful intermediate size, strong enough to hold book shelves. If you will be storing very heavy objects, a larger size will be needed. The pipe comes in 8-foot, 10-foot, 12-foot, and 14-foot lengths. Not all stores stock all the different sizes in all the different lengths. A good place to find this pipe is at discount building supply stores, the kind for do-it-yourselfers. They also stock the fittings and other materials you will need.

The systems shown are assembled using standard fittings. These include caps, L's, T's, X's. There are others as well, but those are the easiest to find. (See Fig. 43.)

In designing a pipe shelf system, keep in mind that you'll need bracing along the length as well as the width. The length bracing can be accomplished by running a length of pipe centered under a shelf. There should be at least two lengthwise braces, one near the top and the other at the bottom. (See Figs. 44 and 45.)

Fastening the shelves to the pipe will reduce the tendency to rack, but will not eliminate it, so the length bracing is recommended.

The first steps in building this system will be to design the unit and make a materials list. Total up the number of feet of pipe you will need and count up the fittings. You will also need a can of special cleaner that helps the solvent "weld" the pipe together, and a can of the welding solvent. The solvent works by slightly melting the pipe and fitting, and as the solvent dries it leaves the pieces solidly fastened together. This is a fast process, usually requiring only a few minutes to be solid.

When you are ready to start cutting, you must allow for the space taken up by the fittings. You can tabulate that distance by measuring inside the fitting to the first ridge. (See Fig. 46) That distance may vary between different types of fitting (like between a T and an X), but will not vary between two fittings of the same type.

The pipe can be cut using an ordinary hand saw, the finer the teeth the better. A mitre box is recommended to help keep the cuts square. The end

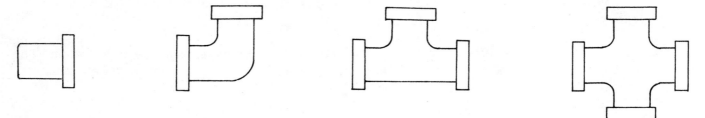

Figure 43   Pipe fittings.

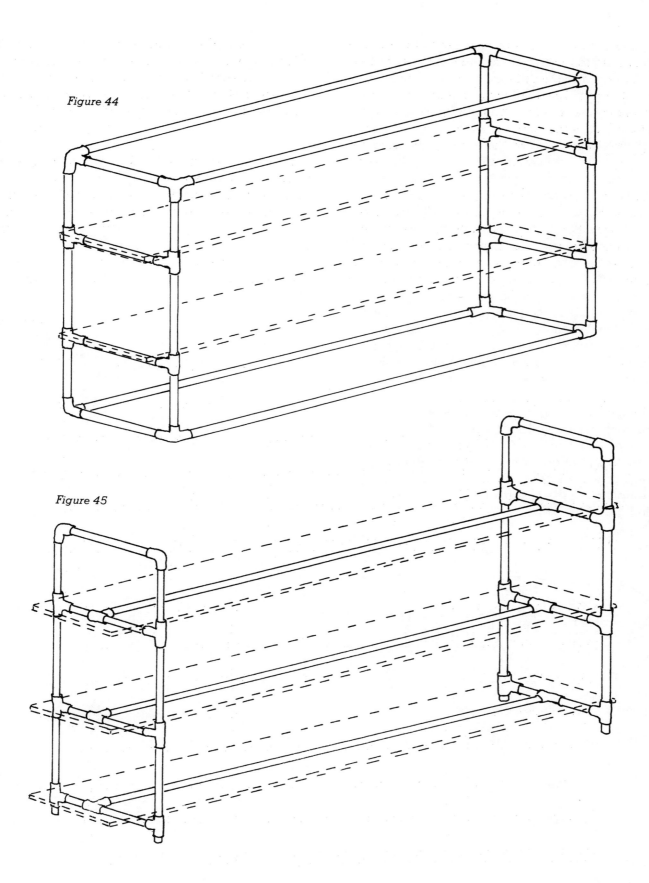

Figure 44

Figure 45

after each cut will need to have the burrs removed. Use emery cloth or a file for this. If you use emery cloth, be sure you clean away the grit left behind, as this grit can interfere with the solvent joint (by leaving gaps) and the welding will not be as strong.

Follow the directions on the can of welding solvent for the correct procedure to follow in welding, but keep in mind that those directions are for making pressure-tight seals in water pipes. Therefore, you can use less solvent and minimize the chance of solvent squeezing out and spoiling a surface that will be visible. You will still get a very strong joint if you use the solvent sparingly.

After you have cut all the pieces to length, simply clean the ends of the pipes with the cleaner and apply the cement. Working quickly, align and assemble each part until the assemblage is complete. The next step would be to put the shelves on—they can be wood, plexi, glass, what have you. The shelves (except glass) can be attached to the pipe by drilling holes in the shelves and pipes and then bolting. (Glass shelves are fastened using double-faced foam tape.) Drill using a regular high-speed drill, but go slightly slower for PVC than for metal or wood to keep the heat low. This will force the drill to cut the hole rather than melt its way through.

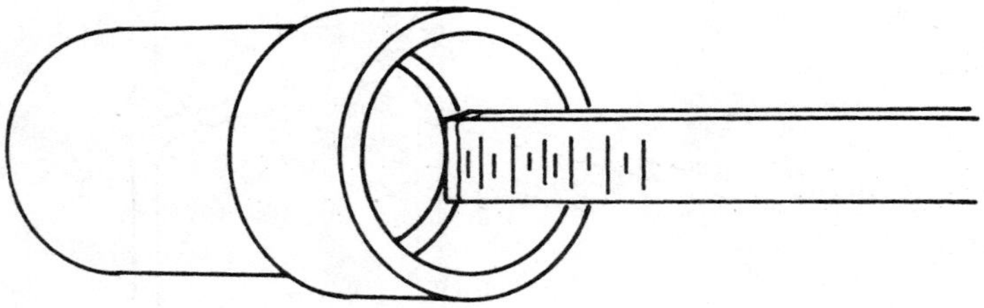

Figure 46   Measure to the first ridge.

Pole and Cross-Piece Shelves

This system of shelves is simple to build, quite attractive, and strong. There is a choice of two types of upright poles: metal or wood.

Wood uprights can be either 2 × 2's , 1-inch (minimum) dowels, or hardwood pieces no less than 1-1/4 by 1-1/4 inches. This is an arbitrary choice of size, but should be well within the strength limitations of the materials.

You can also choose either pipe or tubing. (The difference between pipe and tubing, incidently, is that pipe is produced for carrying liquids or gasses under pressure; tubing may be used for this purpose, but that is not its primary intention.) Pipe and tubing come in many different materials. You can select from PVC (plastic) pipe, aluminum, stainless steel, and others. The "others" will be determined by materials that are available to you locally. Check your *Yellow Pages* under three headings: Plumbing Supplies, Pipe, Tubing.

Some guidelines for selecting pipe or tubing are below. You will find that pipe and tubing come in standard lengths from 6 feet to 16 feet in 2-foot increments. You will find that few suppliers carry all lengths and that the longer lengths are more common than the shorter ones.

In choosing PVC pipe, an O.D. (outer diameter) of 1 inch is about the minimum. Thinner O.D.'s tend to be too flexible. Look the pipe over carefully and make your best estimate as to the diameter that will be strong enough and will still give you the appearance that you want.

Aluminium tubing should be of the "thick wall" variety, and the 1 inch O.D. guideline should be followed. Thin wall and thick wall refer to the thickness of the metal used to make the tube. I have specified thick wall so that the tubing will not collapse or dent as you tighten down on the shelf supports.

Stainless steel will be the most expensive of all the materials mentioned. It is also the strongest and will not rust or require much care. Stainless is the hardest material to cut, and cannot normally be cut with a "tubing cutter," as can others mentioned. It can, however, be cut with a hack saw—or your dealer *may* be willing to cut it for you.

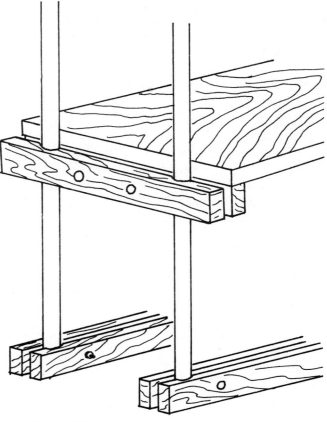

Figure 47

A tubing cutter is a very useful tool in working with pipe or tubing. It makes clean, straight cuts more easily than a saw. Tubing cutters are not very expensive (between $5 and $10) and are available with different blades for different materials. Check with your hardware person.

The shelf supports are made of wood—pine, hardwood, or particle (composition) board. Plywood is generally not suitable because its laminations interfere with the required drilling.

The design is the first step. Determine how wide and how long you want the shelves to be, and what size pipe or tubing you will use. Some guidelines to follow: (1) if your span will be more than 5 feet, use center supports; (2) if the materials you will be storing or displaying are very heavy, choose a pipe or tube 1 inch O.D. or greater.

For the purposes of this explanation, let's say that you will be making the shelves 12 inches wide and will be using 1 inch O.D. PVC pipe. Here is how to proceed:

Each shelf is held up by *shelf supports*. Each support is actually two pieces of wood bolted together that squeeze the tubing to hold itself and the shelf in place (see Fig. 47.). To make the shelf supports, first determine where you will drill the holes that allow the tubing to pass through. Under no circumstances should the holes be less than 1 inch from the end of the support. This will insure that the area around the hole is rigid. The holes should be 1/4 inch *smaller* than the outer diameter of the

pipe or tubing. In our example, the holes will be 3/4 inch and drilled 1-3/8 inches from the end. The latter dimension was determined by adding the 1 inch (minimum from the end of the support) to one-half the diameter of the hole. Clamp the pieces together and drill.

If you are using center uprights in the middle of a long span, remember that the shelves can rest on both sides of the supports.(See Fig. 49.)

In addition to the shelf supports, you will also need supports lengthwise to hold the poles in place and prevent racking. 1 × 2's drilled in the same manner as the shelf supports will be fine. You will need at least four — two at the top (front and rear) and two at the bottom (front and rear).

After the shelf supports have been drilled to allow the poles to pass through them, they will need to be drilled for the bolts that will hold them tight. The bolts I chose are carriage bolts, the ones with the smooth round heads (Fig. 50). These will give a clean appearance. They should be installed so that the nuts are under the shelves, leaving the heads on the outside. Either 1/4 or 5/16 inch is a suitable size.

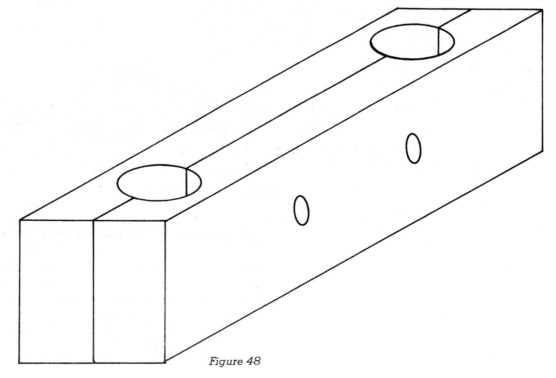

Figure 48

With the supports clamped together as before, drill the bolt holes about 1 inch inside the pole holes, in the other plane (see Fig. 48.) I recommend washers on the nut-side of the bolt between the nut itself and the wood. No washer is needed on the head side. If you think you will want to move the shelves very often, wing- or thumb-nuts can be used.

To assemble the units, install crutch tips on the bottom of the pipes or tubes (optional). Then bolt on and tighten up the lengthwise supports so that the unit will stand on its own. Next, begin installing the shelf supports and the shelves. The bolts should be tightened enough so that the supports hold firmly, but not so tight that they might collapse the pipes or tubes.

Figure 49

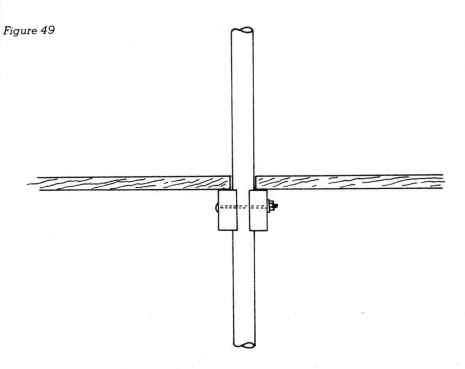

Figure 50

All Wood Shelves

In building wood shelving units, you'll need to consider a number of factors. First is how large the shelves will be, where they will be (do they need to be decorative?) and what will be stored or displayed on them. Once you have a rough idea of what your shelves will look like, choose the materials you will use—pine, plywood, particle board, or hardwood.

The next consideration is how the shelves will be supported. Will you want the shelves to be movable up and down or to be fixed in position?

If you want movable shelves, here are two ways you can go about it. First is what I call the "peg system." The peg system is made by drilling parallel tracks of holes in the uprights (on the shelf

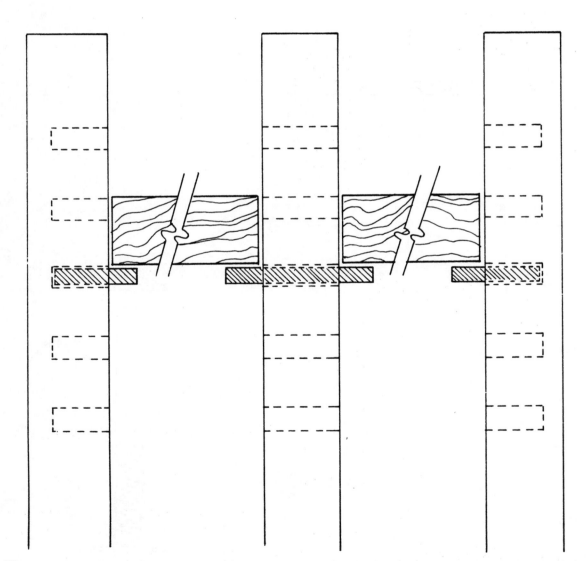

Figure 51

side); they are drilled only part way through on the outside uprights and can be drilled all the way through on the interior uprights in a multi- unit. Pieces of dowel that fit snugly in the holes act as the supports for the shelves. The pegs can be moved up and down into different holes so that the height of the shelves can be changed. I recommend 1/4-inch or 5/16- inch dowels.

A second method of making movable shelves is to use commercially available tracks and clips. In each shelf unit a track with a clip at each corner of the shelf makes shelves movable.

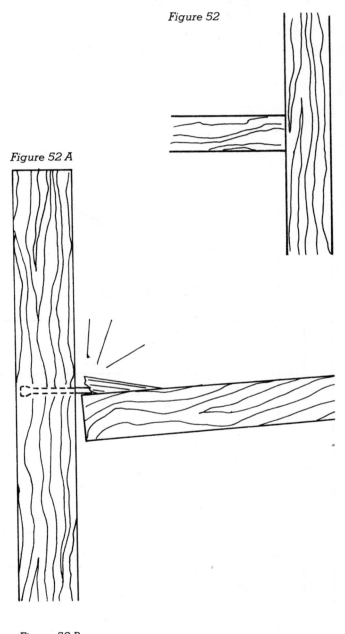

Try using a piece of peg board as a template for drilling the holes.

will be moderate. Too much weight can cause the nail or screw to break through the upper side of the shelf. For this reason, it is necessary as well to make sure the nails or screws are driven straight. Caution: You cannot use this method on plywood shelves because the nails or screws will split the laminations apart and will not hold.

Figure 52

Figure 52 A

Fixed shelves can be done in three ways. There is a fourth but I will cover that one in the last section.

The first and simplest method is to nail or screw the shelves in place using the "butt" method. This method is useful as long as the weight of the shelf

Figure 52 B

The second method uses small shelf supports made of solid wood or particle board (not plywood for the same reason above). The supports should be approximately the same width as the shelf and can be made of 1 × 1 or 1 × 2 material. The supports are screwed into the uprights at a height that is the final height you want the shelf to be less the thickness of the shelf — thus the shelf resting on top of the support will be at the desired height. The shelf rests on the support and can be nailed or screwed to it if desired. This system handles weight easily. (See Fig. 53.)

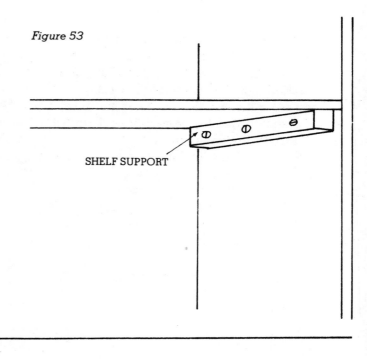

Figure 53

SHELF SUPPORT

Figure 54

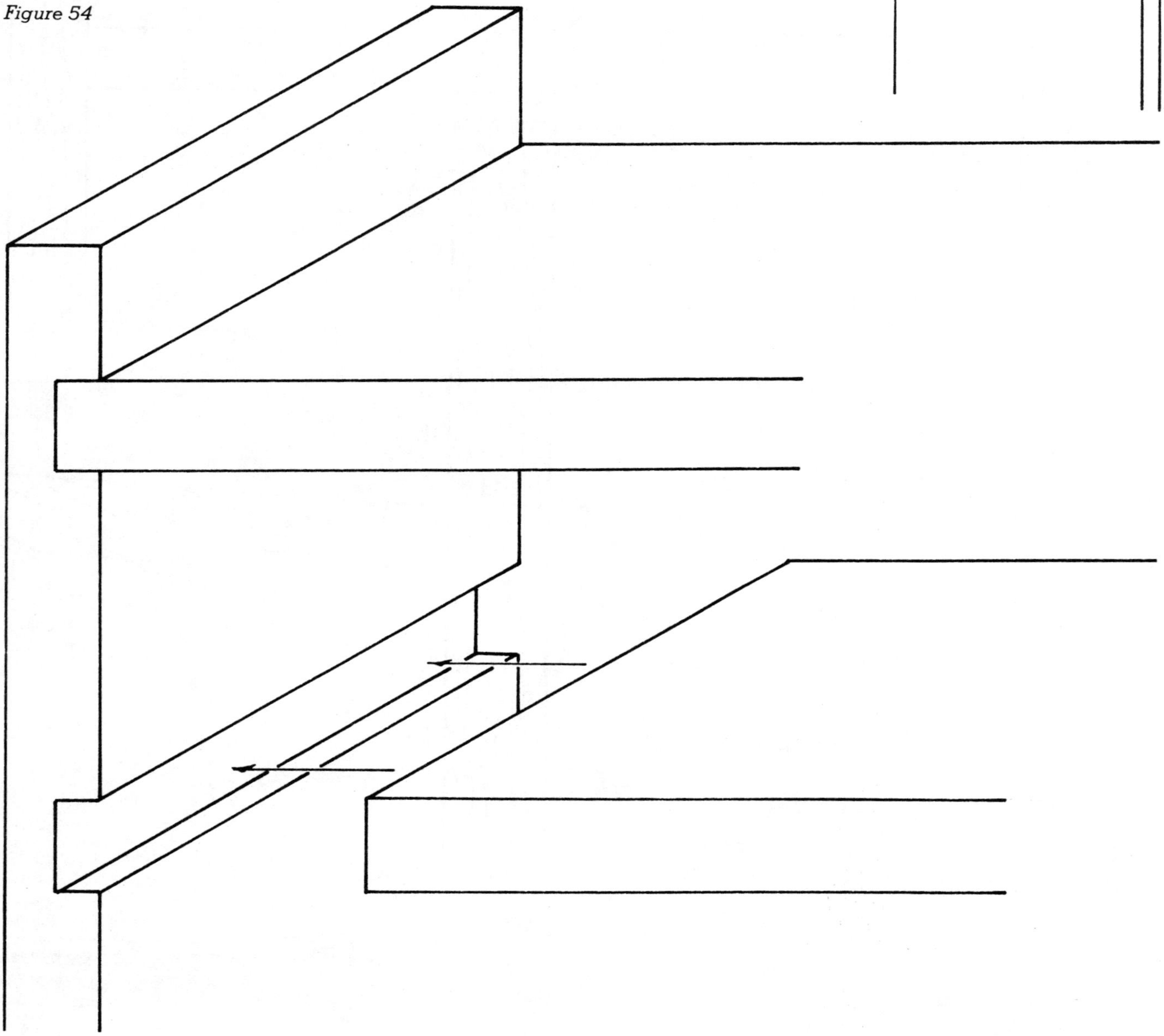

The third method requires the most skills. It is done by plowing out grooves in the uprights for the shelves to fit into. These are called rabbet joints. This method requires that the length of all shelves are nearly exactly the same to insure a tight fit.

The grooves are plowed out using a router (a high-speed tool specifically for this purpose), a radial arm or table saw with special attachments, or by using a chisel and special plane. This is not an undertaking for a novice; and I will assume that the more experienced builder will know the technique, so I won't go into it further. If you don't have experience with rabbets but would like to use them, seek the aid of a friend who knows the technique and get some expert assistance. The instruction booklet that comes with most routers carries full instructions for how-to-do-it. This system handles weight easily.

All of these methods will hold glass or Plexiglas shelves as well, except for the "butt" method for obvious reasons.

To back or not to back, that is the next question. A backing is a large piece(s) of wood that completely covers the back of the unit; it is an ideal way to eliminate racking. There are also, however, ways to make shelves sturdy without a backing and we will look into these as well.

Here is how to make a backing. The backing material is often Masonite (a composition board material made of pressed wood) or thin plywood. You can also use a piece of paneling that matches the wall behind.

The backing is usually a little bit smaller than the overall dimensions of the shelf unit so that it does not extend past the outside edges of the uprights or beyond the top. I recommend that it be cut approximately 1/4 inch shorter than the height from top to bottom and about 1/4 inch shorter than the length left to right. With the unit lying down, the backing is centered and is nailed or screwed in place. If your uprights are made of plywood, use nailing strips to avoid the splitting problem inherent with ply.

Figure 55

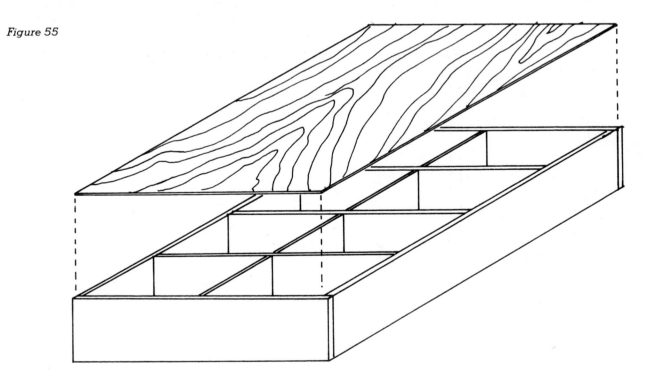

Nail backing in place, using glue and nails for greater strength.

The backing is normally finished in the same color or stain as the rest of the unit, but a contrasting color can be interesting. Another alternative is to paint the backing the same color as the wall it will go up against. This will make it seem to disappear.

An alternative to making a full backing is to use gussetts. A gussett is made using the same material that you would use for backing; it is a small triangle that gets nailed or screwed across the four outside corners of the unit and on the interior joints as needed. (See Fig. 56.)

Alternatives to backing the whole unit are many. I'll cover a few here. I'm sure that there are others, but these are ones I know and am sure of.

An almost free-standing shelf unit without a backing can be built to be sturdy and racking-free. Such a unit makes for a good divider, where the ability to see through is often desirable. One method of accomplishing this is to brace the unit to one wall (Fig. 57). In this method, the top and bottom shelves must be solidly attached to the uprights so that the rest of the unit shares the support of the wall.

If your shelves with no backing are to go parallel to the wall, nailing strips at the top of the unit can be screwed into the studs in the wall, thus making the shelves firm.

Figure 56

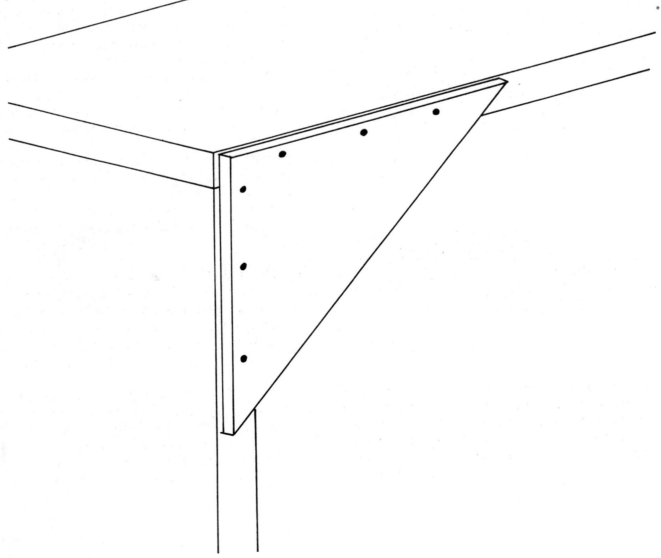

To make a unit that will not be attached to any wall like an island unit, one way to go is to fasten the uprights to the floor *and* the ceiling with the use of nailing strips. With this method, each upright is solidly fastened; the shelves, therefore, need not be solidly attached. Hence this method is ideal with glass or Plexiglas shelves, as well as wood. A "see-through" island with plexi or glass shelves gives a very open feeling.

Another approach that can be used consists of a lower cabinet that supports the shelves above, similar to those seen in furniture stores. However, the cabinet-making and advanced construction techniques needed to build such a unit are beyond the scope of this book.

But do not despair. The fourth method I promised you is free-standing, has no backing, and does not need to be attached to the floor, walls, or ceiling.

I call this method the "Liquor Box Method" because I got the idea from the dividers that hold the bottles apart in a carton of liquor. This method is very strong, resists racking, and can be made quite attractive. Any number of arrangements of shelves and units is possible using this method. Parts of the other methods can be mixed with this one, if the liquor box method is used for the basic structure.

Figure 57

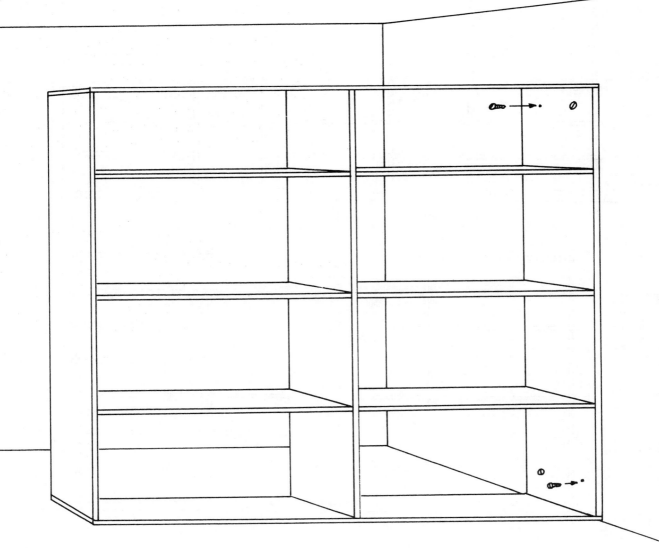

The pieces of this method go together like the dividers in the box. Each piece has a slot cut in it that is one-half its width and as wide as the thickness of the mating piece. The mating piece is similarly cut. The two fit together at right angles, hold firmly. (See Fig. 59.)

The liquor box method works best with plywood. If you use solid wood, the small piece that is on the outside of the slot is subject to splitting; it will often break off and spoil the appearance as well as diminish the strength.

Here are a few tips for using this method. The amount of wood left beyond the slot should not be less than the thickness of the wood being used. The width of the slot should be as close to the thickness of the wood being used as possible. If there will be error, err in the direction of too snug rather than too loose. The length of the slots should be about 1/16 inch longer than one-half the width. Following these tips will assure a tight fit and maximum strength.

No nails, screws, or glue are needed to assemble this system. A block of wood (for pounding on) and a mallet will be all the tools you'll need. Assembly should be easy. I suggest that, if possible, the unit be assembled with it laying on the floor. The pieces are then tapped into place using the mallet and us-

Figure 58

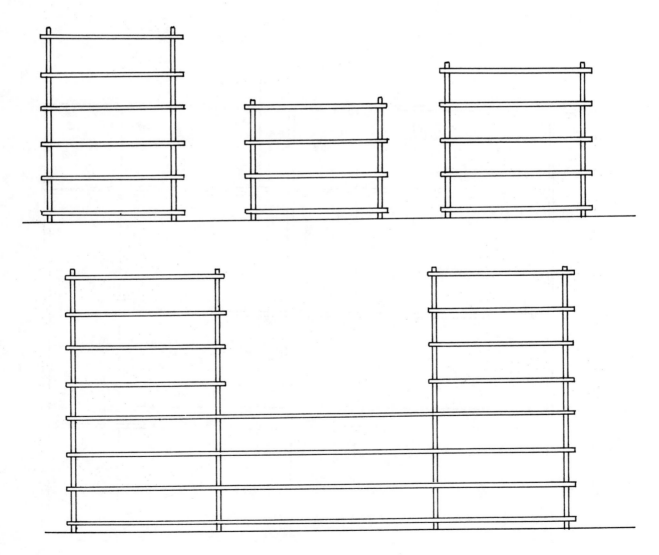

ing the wood block to protect the surfaces you are striking. If for some reason the pieces are a little too snug, rubbing the insides of the slots with bar soap will help them slide more easily. If the soap doesn't remedy the situation, the slots have been cut too narrow and will need to be opened slightly. Again, too tight is MUCH better than too loose.

Once the unit is assembled it is stood up; any finish that you may want can be applied. This system is ideal for people who move frequently since it can be taken apart as easily as it is put together and can thus be transported flat.

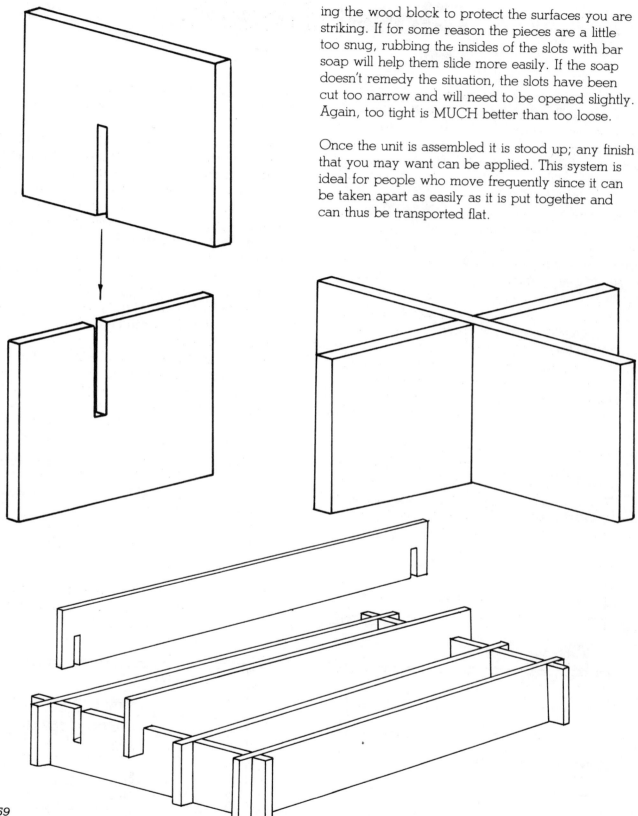

Figure 59

Closet Shelves

Adding shelves to a closet is often easy because there are walls inside the closet that can be used for supporting the shelves. The inside of closets in most homes is of plaster or drywall construction, so be sure to follow the instructions for fastening to these materials.

The illustrations in Figure 60 show several ways a closet can be divided to gain more storage space. There are, of course, many other possible arrangements, but you may be able to use some of these ideas as a starting point for your own designs. You can vary the height of the shelves, their length or width, even slant them for holding special items like shoes, wine, or tools, or adjust them to suit more specific needs such as space for a card table, your bowling ball, and so on.

The existing "hat shelf" in most closets is made from 12- inch pine, so this material is ideal for additional shelving. You can also use plywood or particle board cut into 12- inch-wide strips.

I'll cover below the way to go about building the unit shown that divides the closet in half. The method for this will apply to other designs with little modification.

The first step, as always, is to look the closet over and decide on a design. Figure out as exactly as possible what you want to store—and be sure to consider how bulky items will fit through the door. If you want the shelves to be movable, use the "peg system" or "tracks and clips" (pp. 56–57). A slanted shelf for shoes can be useful.

Make a sketch of your design, measure the dimensions you will need, and mark them on your drawing. A trick for making accurate inside measurements is to put two yardsticks together with

Figure 60

rubber bands and add the total on one to 36 inches to get the total inside distance. Keep in mind that the molding around the floor (if any) will have to be taken into consideration. Notching out the bottom of the uprights will overcome this difficulty. (See Fig. 62.)

Figure 62

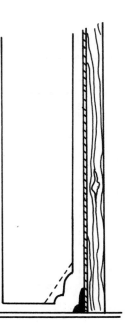

After you have the design and measurements, cut the wood or have it cut at the lumberyard. You will need: upright(s), shelves, nailing strips (to fasten the uprights to the floor and ceiling or hat shelf), nails, screws, and a little luck. Remove anything in the closet that will get in your way, like the existing clothes bar, hooks, etc. There is nothing quite so unpleasant as catching your head on a coat hook!

Gather the materials together and cut or have the yard cut all the pieces you'll need. With all the materials to hand, a trial fit is next. First test the upright(s) in place. Seldom is a floor perfectly level, so a little adjusting is usually required. If the upright is too short or doesn't sit flat, small bits of wood under it will make it snug or steady. If the upright is too long, a little may have to be trimmed off. If the upright pushes up the hat shelf just a little (1/8 inch or less), don't bother to trim it unless it makes the hat shelf too unstable.

Next, trial fit the shelves with the upright(s) in place. Test a shelf at both the top and the bottom of the upright. When you see how it will all fit together and are sure the parts are the right size, make a pencil mark on the floor to show you where the nailing strip will be fastened. The strip can go on either side of the upright, but I recommend that it be on the side "away" from the shelves. This will give you a more solid base to drive screws against.

The nailing strip should be screwed into the floor rather than nailed because most floors are hardwood (oak, maple, etc.) and nails will often bounce off or bend. Screws will hold, though first you should drill a pilot hole (a small hole less than the diameter of the screw to remove some of the wood which the screw would have had to cut through). Knowing the correct size for pilot holes is important for driving screws in hard wood. If the hole is too large the screw will not hold well; if it is too small the screw will shear off while trying to drive it. A chart showing the correct sizes for pilot holes can be found on page 22.

Now it is time to install the lower nailing strip for the upright. If you are using more than one upright, put all the nailing strips in at this point.

The next step will be to install the upper nailing strip. This is done in the same way as the lower one: trial fit the upright; check its location using a shelf; mark the hat shelf or ceiling; and, install the nailing strip. Note that the hat shelf is softwood usually (pine), so use the softwood pilot-hole size from the chart. (To test if you have hardwood or soft, press your fingernail into the wood in an inconspicuous place. If you can make a dent easily, the wood is soft; if the wood will not dent easily or if the dent is no deeper than a scratch, the wood is hard.) Now actually install the nailing strip.

Now, screw the uprights in place. Two screws at the top and two at the bottom will usually be adequate. Be sure in driving the screws that you do not run into the screws used to secure the nailing strips to the floor or hat shelf.

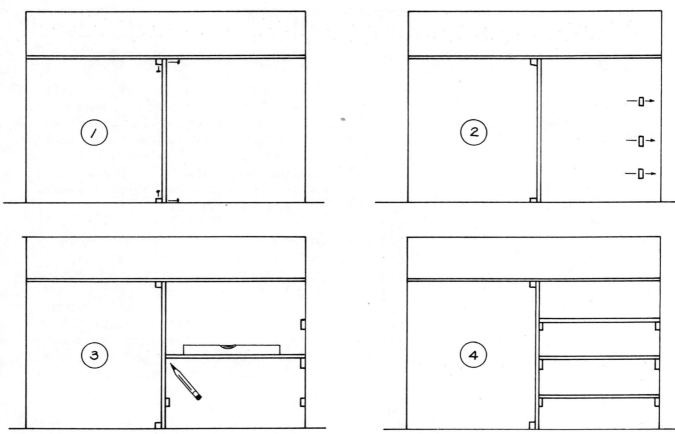

Figure 63

Figure 63 A

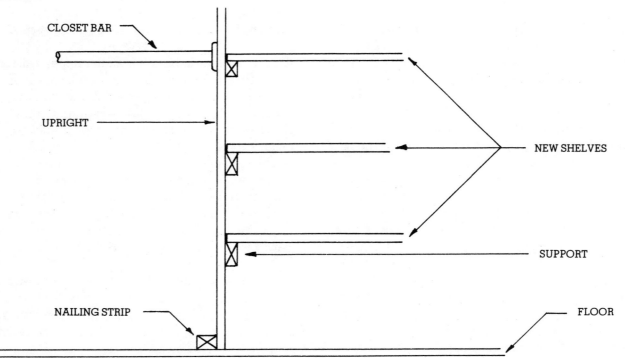

CLOSET BAR

UPRIGHT

NEW SHELVES

SUPPORT

NAILING STRIP

FLOOR

66

With the uprights in place, measure off and mark the heights of the shelves. Install the supports for the shelves on one side only (the wall side if possible). Then, using a level, rest the bottom shelf on the support; watching the level as it sits on the shelf, raise or lower the shelf until it is level. When it is level, mark the other upright along the bottom of the shelf. This will mark the top edge of the support for that side. Do the same with each shelf in sequence. When all are marked, install all the supports on that side. Slide the shelves in place and nail them down with finishing nails if you like (optional). Closet bars, hooks, etc. can now be reinstalled.

If you are interested in making shoe racks or other slanted shelves, take a look at Figure 64. The only difference between these and the level shelves is that the supports are installed at an angle. The angle for shoes that works well is that created by a 4-to-6 inch rise, front to back. A quick test with a few shoes will show the right slant. Follow the method of nailing first one side, fitting the shelf in place, marking the opposite upright, and installing the other support. A level won't be much help, but you can do a pretty good job by eye. A length of a small trim wood (e.g., 1/2 × 1/2) can be nailed to the shelf and hook under the heels of the shoes to keep them from sliding off. The shelves themselves should be nailed in place to keep them from sliding off the supports.

It is easy to add a second hat shelf for some out-of-the-way storage or for seldom-used articles. Simply duplicate the existing hat shelf. If you plan to store heavy objects, such as boxes of books, a center support should be added to keep the shelves from collapsing. A 1 × 2 run from the center of the new shelf to the floor is an easy solution. A small nailing strip at the floor will keep it from being kicked out, and it should be nailed to both the new shelf and the existing shelf for best strength. (See Fig. 65.)

If your closet has an alcove, you can easily fill that alcove with shelves. This method can also be used if you want to fill an ordinary closet with shelves wall-to-wall. Use the 1 × 2 method to support the shelves simply by fastening 1 × 2's to the walls at the height you want the shelves. Pine shelving or any type of wood can be used for the shelves

themselves, and the pine can be put side-by-side to gain more width if desired. As before, use a center support if the shelves will carry a great deal of weight.

Figure 64

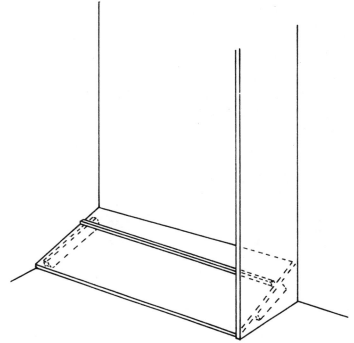

A single nailing strip along the rear edge will also work.

Figure 65

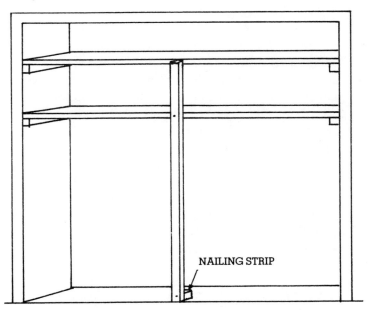

NAILING STRIP

Inside-the-Door Shelves

Inside-the-door shelves work well on closet doors as well as basement doors, bathroom doors, pantry doors, etc. In the design of this type of shelf system, five factors should be considered.

The first is the depth of the shelves. As the door opens, the radius created by the maximum depth nearest the hinges will have to be allowed for so that the shelves do not collide with things inside the closet. (See Fig. 66.)

Figure 66

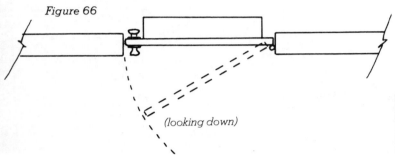

(looking down)

The second factor is the distance of the shelf from the doorknob-side of the door. Again, check the radius created by the depth of the shelf so it will not collide with the door frame and prevent the door from being opened or closed.

The third factor is weight. The shelf unit plus its contents will increase the weight on the hinges of the door. So check to make sure that the screws are solidly in both the frame and the door. If there is any question, replace the existing screws with ones 1/2 inch longer. Check also that the hinges themselves can take the extra weight. If you have any doubts, replace them with stronger ones. If you have any doubts that the door can itself handle the extra weight, it becomes a judgment call. Any specific way that I might advise would get me into trouble with someone, so I suggest that you call a friend whose observations are pretty often accurate and get a second opinion.

The fourth factor is whether your door is solid or hollow. A few raps with your knuckles will tell you the difference. If the door sounds the same as the frame when you rap it, it is a solid door; if it doesn't, then it's hollow. Solid doors are usually made with a thick framework and thinner panel inserts. Keep in mind that fastening to the solid door should be done only on the thick framework; screws long enough to get a secure grip would go all the way through the thinner panels and spoil the opposite side of the door. In a hollow door, we will use a special fastener (called a hollow-door Molly bolt), so the shelving unit can be placed almost anywhere on the door.

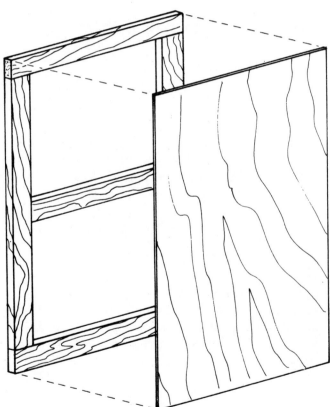

Figure 67   **Inside a hollow door.**

The fifth factor is holding the objects on the shelves. Because the shelves move with the door, retaining strips (Fig. 68) will be needed to keep items from falling off.

A finished unit is shown in Figure 68. No braces are required to prevent racking because the door serves as the backing. The shelf arrangement can be varied a lot and can include bins or baskets, runs for holding can goods, etc.

The actual fastening to the door can be a little tricky. Here is a sure-fire method I have used (there may be others). The first step is to attach screw eyes into the side supports of the shelves near the top and the bottom, four total.

In a hollow door we will fasten the screw eyes to the door using hollow-door Molly bolts. Your hardware person can show you the right ones. DO NOT use plastic anchors, as these will not hold and will probably pull the wood of the door apart or split it. With the Molly bolts to hand, prop the shelf unit up on a box or chair and mark the door through the screw eyes with a pencil. Drill the hole needed for the Mollys (the Molly-bolt package will tell you the correct size) and install the Mollys according to the directions. Remove the screws, prop the unit back up again, and replace the screws. You are done.

The same procedure is used for a solid door except that No. 8 or No. 10 round-head wood screws are used instead of Mollys. You may have to use washers if the heads of the screws will pass through the eyes of the screw eyes. A little soap on the threads of the screws and attention to the correct size of the pilot hole (see Fig. 14) will make driving the screws a lot easier.

These units can be hung anywhere—not just on doors—so keep an eye open for other applications.

Figure 68

It may be necessary to put retaining strips on the front of the shelves to keep things from falling off.

RETAINING STRIPS

(RUBBER BANDS, SMALL STRIPS OF WOOD, OR LIGHTWEIGHT CHAIN)

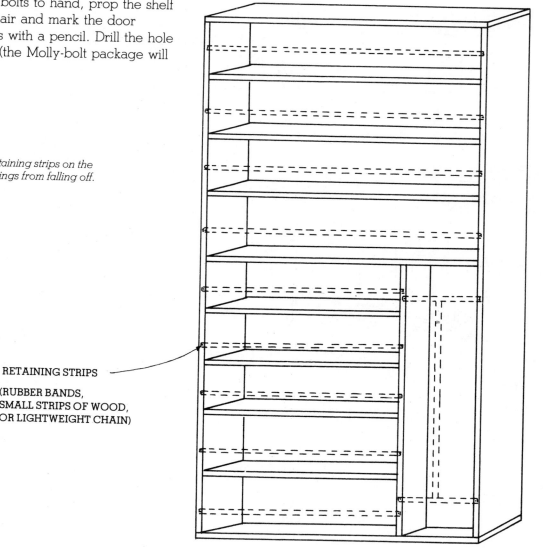

The Recycled Box System

Ecologists, take heart. Here is a shelf system that uses existing wooden crates or boxes—vegetable boxes, liquor crates, any kind of wooden box. I admit that in this age of cardboard, wooden boxes are not easy to find; but if you have a source, this system is for you.

Take a look at it upside-down, too!

Figure 69

No source? You can build your own boxes easily and inexpensively. Since this system tends to be "rustic" in appearance, the rougher and cheaper woods work fine for the boxes. If you don't want the rustic appearance, you can use higher quality wood, of course.

Cheap wood can often be found just lying around outside a lumberyard. The wood is often badly weathered (ideal) and sometimes free for the asking. You'll be surprised how much you can find.

The illustration (Fig. 70) shows how the boxes are assembled. Use nails or screws to hold them together, and keep it simple. You may or may not want to put a backing on the boxes, depending on whether or not you wish to be able to see the wall through them.

Fastening the boxes to the wall should be relatively simple. If the boxes have backs, they can be screwed into the studs or attached with Molly bolts.

If the boxes have no back, a strip of wood inset into the rear of the box is screwed to the studs or Molly-bolted to the wall as before.

The boxes are assembled and mounted from the floor (or lowest one) to the top. Spaces left between boxes will form a shelf without an extra box. The boxes can be nailed to one another for extra rigidity as you go along.

If you plan to put something quite heavy (like a TV set) in or on one of the boxes, angle irons should be installed in the corners of the box to give it extra strength. Be sure that any such box with a lot of weight is strong enough to carry it, and remember that fastening it to a stud is essential.

Figure 70

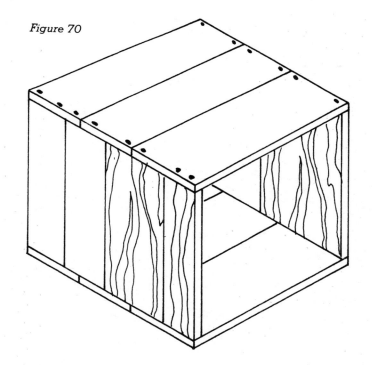

Stagger wide and narrow boards.

Back-to-Back Shelves

The following system will make a free-standing set of shelves that can be used as a room divider without any backing. The system can be built in two basic configurations: with shelves on one side (with the shelves touching a wall) or with shelves on both sides (free standing, providing that the weight difference from one side to the other is reasonable—say, within 150 pounds). The system is designed to go from floor to ceiling, but if made shorter it can stand on top of another piece of furniture as well.

This shelf system is a mixture of hardware-store items and do-it-yourself pieces. The construction work is rather simple, but some degree of precision is required for excellent results.

The backbone of the system is the wooden upright. Uprights are made from what is called "five-quarter stock," that is, wood that is 1-1/4 inches square. Metal shelf standards are fastened to one side or

Figure 71

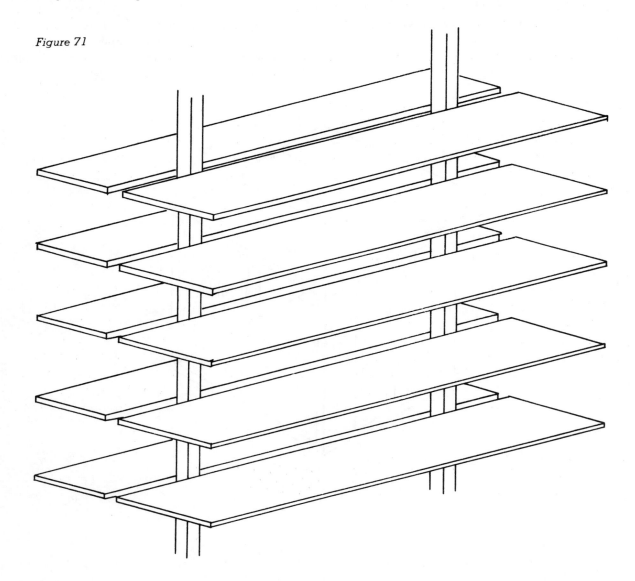

two opposite sides of the uprights. The uprights are completely free standing and are held securely between the floor and the ceiling with a spring "tensioner" which you make yourself.

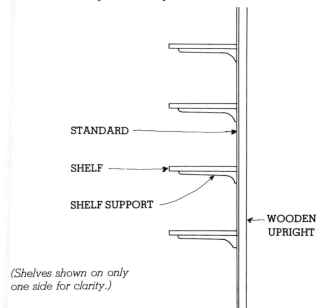

STANDARD

SHELF

SHELF SUPPORT

← WOODEN UPRIGHT

(Shelves shown on only one side for clarity.)

To determine how many uprights you will need, you should allow a maximum span of 32 inches. Less would be better but not essential. With the 32-inch span, a three-foot shelf would overhang 2 inches on each end—ideal. Regardless of the span you decide on, a 2-inch overhang should be maintained.

After you determine how many uprights you'll need, the next step is to determine their length. Measure the distance from the ceiling to the floor in the location that the shelves will be. This distance minus 4-1/2 inches will be their length. (Note: for a room with exposed beams, the uprights may be bolted directly to the beams. This will mean that the length of the uprights will be the height from floor to ceiling less 2 inches rather than 4-1/2.)

The uprights, lengths of dowel, and shelving material can be bought from the lumberyard. The uprights are made from CLEAR pine—no knots. The reason is that the area around a knot is not as strong as the rest of the board; this could eventually cause the upright to break.

For the uprights you will have two choices of material: five-quarter stock, or baluster stock (the wood used for banisters and the like). Whichever one you choose should be approximately 1-1/4 inches square.

The choice between five-quarter or baluster stock is made on the basis of straightness. You will find that the baluster stock will always be almost dead-straight, but it is a lot more expensive than five-quarter. So look over the supply of five-quarter to see if you can find suitable pieces and save yourself some money.

You will need 9 inches of dowel to use with each upright. (The lengths of the dowel were chosen so that you could get all the dowel needed for four uprights from one 3-foot length.) The dowel is 1/2 inch diameter. You will also need two crutch tips for each upright, the 1/2-inch size, which will fit on the dowels. Select white if you can; it will not mark floors or ceilings.

The first step of construction is to cut the uprights to the proper length. Once cut, it is time to drill in each end the holes that the dowels will fit into. The hole at the bottom is drilled into the end of the upright 2 inches deep. Take care to see that the hole goes straight into the wood. A piece of tape on the shank of the drill bit will help you keep the depths uniform from one piece to the next. (Measure up from the widest point of the drill.) Drill all the lower holes at one time. (See Figure 72.)

Figure 72

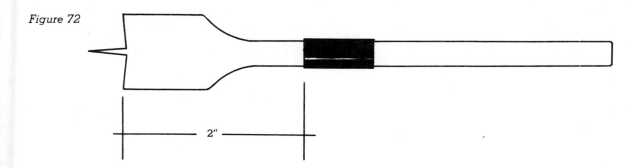

2"

The upper holes are drilled in the same way; their depth is 5 inches. Mark the drill shank with a piece of tape as before. Note: if you are bolting your uprights to open ceiling beams, the upper holes are not needed.

When all the holes are drilled, cut the dowels. You will need two pieces for each upright, one 4 inches long for the lower hole, one 5 inches long for the upper hole.

The lower dowel is fitted into the hole and glued with white glue (like Elmer's, for example).

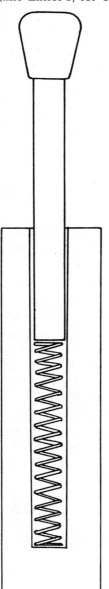

Figure 73

The upper (5-inch) piece is *not* glued. It must move freely in and out of the hole as it will have a spring under it that will push against the ceiling. If it is too snug, run the drill in and out of the hole a few times to enlarge it. You can also sand the dowel with sandpaper to get a little extra clearance if needed. (See Figure 73.)

The spring can usually be found at a good hardware store. Keep in mind that the spring must be the type that can be compressed and so pushes the dowel against the ceiling. The spring should be about 3 inches in length and should be fairly strong. Put the spring in the hole and test with the dowel. If the dowel is still a little reluctant to slide freely, rub it all over with regular bar soap or candle wax. This will act as a lubricant and should smooth up its operation. If the soap or wax doesn't help, the hole will need further enlarging or the dowel will need further sanding.

The standards and brackets are ordinary hardware-store items. You can choose the decorative types if you like. You will need to use the 72-inch lengths for the floor to ceiling uprights; obviously shorter lengths are required for shorter uprights. You also will need enough brackets to support the shelves.

Install the standards on the uprights. If you are making the shelves back-to-back, you will need to install standards on two opposite sides of the upright. If you will have shelves on one side only, then you will need only one standard on each upright. (See Figure 74.)

Finally, install the crutch tips on all the dowels. Drop the spring into the upper hole and insert the upper dowel on top of it. A useful tip for putting the uprights in place is to push the upper end into the ceiling and compress the spring while sliding the lower end into position. If for some reason the tension is inadequate, put a small block of wood under the spring inside the upper hole. If the tension is too great, then cut a *short* section off the upper dowel (1/4 inch to start, more later if needed). Fit one upright at a time. Because one is too tight or too loose does not necessarily mean that the others will be also. Variations in the ceiling can be a bit tricky.

Install the shelves and the job is done. See the "Planning and Design" section for tips on finishing the wood.

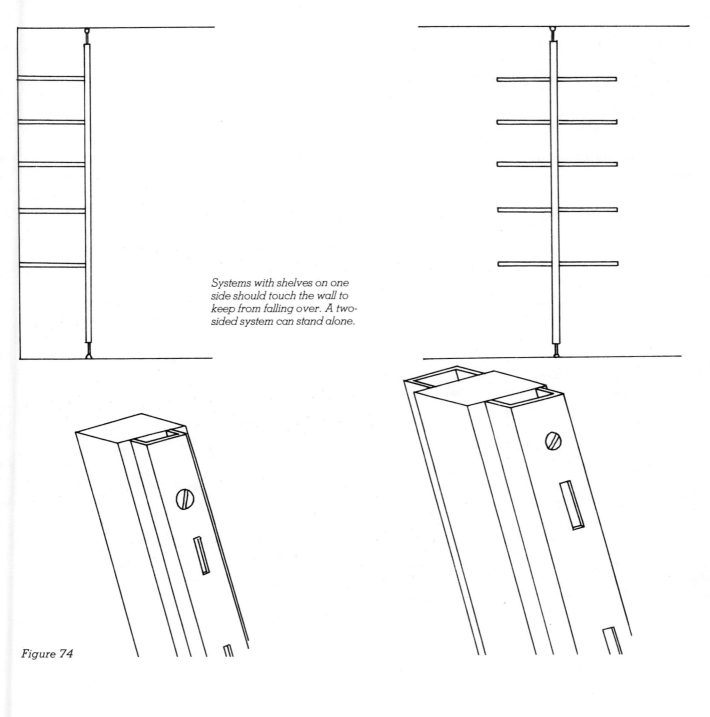

Systems with shelves on one side should touch the wall to keep from falling over. A two-sided system can stand alone.

Figure 74

Heavy-Duty Peg System

Here is an idea for shelves that can be very attractive, easy to build, and easy to put up. The heavy-duty peg system can hold a lot of weight for a decorative shelving system and has a rustic, solid look.

The shelves rest on 3/4-inch dowels that are fit into 2 × 10's fastened to the wall. A special method of securing the dowels ensures that they never pull free.

The 2 × 10's can be any height you choose; however, they should be at least 6 inches taller than the height of the top shelf to make sure that the dowels supporting the top shelf do not pull out or break their way out.

The 2 × 10 uprights will support almost any number of shelves. Using this system, there is virtually no limit to the arrangements that can be created.

Figure 75

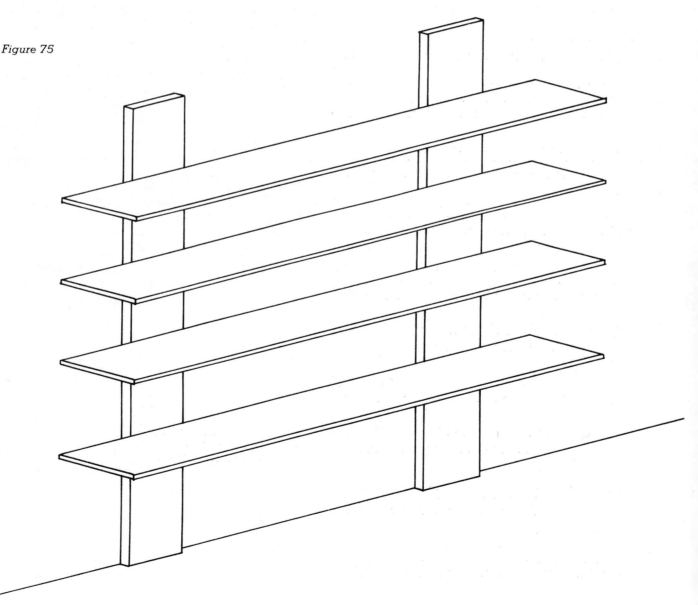

The uprights are drilled at the points where you want the shelves. All the holes in the uprights for any given shelf must be in the same location so that the shelf will rest level. The holes are drilled in the uprights to accept the 3/4-inch dowel shelf supports; the uprights should be drilled all the way through. The dowel supports must fit snugly into these holes, so I recommend drilling with an 11/16-inch bit and forcing the dowels in.

To install the dowels, coat the insides of the holes with white glue and tap the dowels in place. If they are too snug, sand the outside of the dowels down a bit with sandpaper. If the shelves will be carrying a lot of weight, such as plants, electronic equipment, etc., use the special procedure that follows. (If they will be mostly decorative, carrying light weight, the extra step will not be needed.)

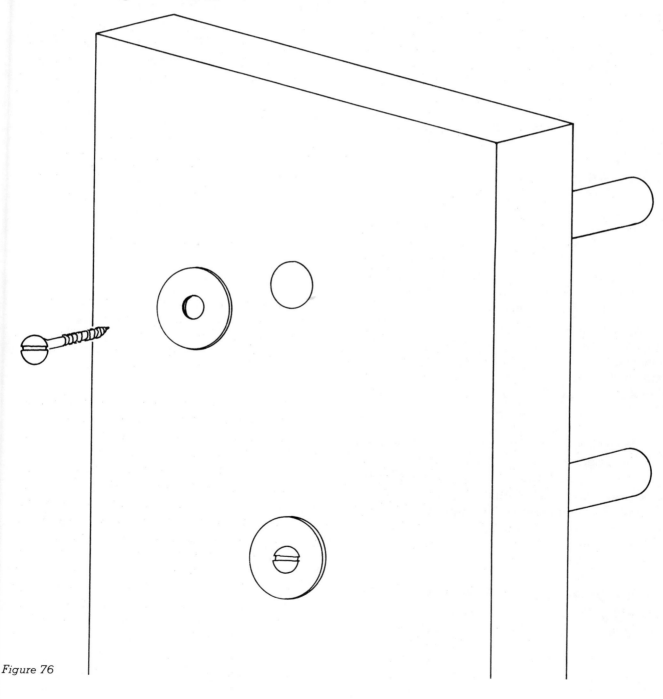

Figure 76

For absolute certainty that the dowels will never pull out, the end of each dowel is drilled with a pilot hole to accept a 1-1/4-inch No. 8 flat-head wood screw. A fender washer with an outside diameter of 1 or 1-1/2 inches is slipped over the screw, and the screw is driven into the dowel. While the screw expands the dowel inside the hole, increasing its hold, the fender washer prevents the dowel from pulling out. If you use this screw-and-washer method, gluing is optional, but recommended.

The shelves in the peg system can be made to be adjustable, provided that the weight is not so great that it wrenches the pegs out. To make them movable, drill the holes for the dowels equally spaced along the entire length of the 2 × 10 uprights, about 4 inches apart. The shelves can be moved just by changing the location of the dowels and reinstalling the shelf.

Fastening the uprights to the walls is best done by locating the studs in the walls and driving 5-inch-long No. 10 wood screws through the uprights and into the studs. (For instructions on how to find a stud, see the "Fastening and Hanging" section.) Place the uprights up against the wall, centered on the line of the stud; check to see that the upright is vertical, and drill a pilot hole through the upright and on into the wall. Do this for the four screws (minimum) that will hold each upright in place. Once all the holes are drilled, remove the upright from against the wall and drill a little deeper into the holes which have been started in the studs.

Coat the screws with soap and drive the first screw into the upright until the screw protrudes about 1 inch out the back. Locate the hole in the wall that corresponds to that screw and maneuver the board into place. Drive the screw home and proceed with the remainder of the screws. (If for some reason studs are unavailable, see the alternatives in the "Fastening and Hanging" section.)

Note that by securing to the studs, an ideal span is created from one support to the other—32 inches—exactly the distance center to center between every other stud.

The shelves per se are made from pine, plywood, particle board, or hardwood, 3/4-inch thick.

Finishing these shelves can be done just like on any others. However, there is a way of finishing these that I am particularly fond of. Stain the 2 × 10's a dark brown color (like walnut) and paint the shelves and dowels white. This makes the dowels almost invisible while the dark brown 2 × 10's are visually striking in any room.

Any lumber-mill marks in the 2 × 10's can be removed with sandpaper before finishing.

No Visible Means of Support

Here is a shelf system that hangs from the wall with no brackets or supports visible. The system is based on a device called "pinch blocks."

Pinch blocks consist of two pieces of wood, each cut at a 45-degree angle along one edge. One of the blocks is secured to the wall; the other becomes part of the structure of the shelf. See Figure 77.

The blocks are made from 1 × 3's. For best support, the blocks should be the full length of the shelves. Since the 45-degree cut can be a little tricky, it is best made with a power saw of some kind. A sabre saw that has a provision for adjusting the angle of the sole plate will do an adequate job; a table saw or radial arm saw is better. If you don't have the tools needed, get a friend (or the lumberyard) to make the cut for you. A clean, accurate cut will allow a tight fit when the job is completed, and a tight fit is important to ensure a strong shelf.

These shelves are made to appear somewhat thicker in order to completely hide the pinch bar. The construction details are shown in Figure 78.

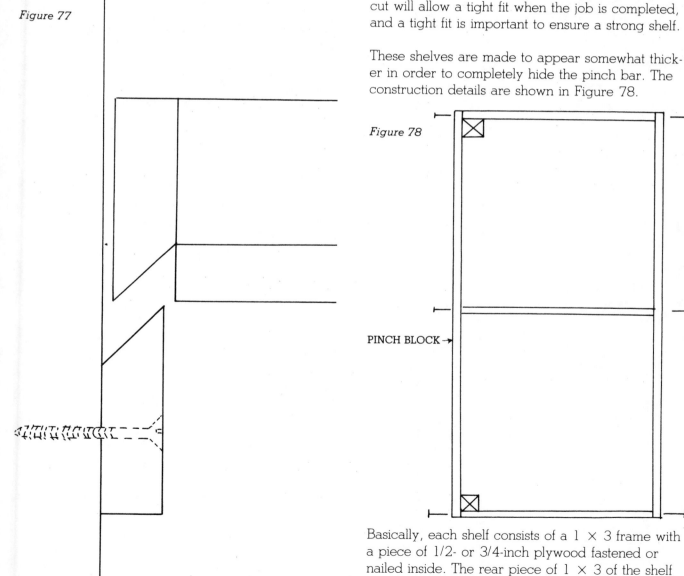

Figure 77

Figure 78

PINCH BLOCK →

Basically, each shelf consists of a 1 × 3 frame with a piece of 1/2- or 3/4-inch plywood fastened or nailed inside. The rear piece of 1 × 3 of the shelf frame is one half of the pinch bar assembly.

The other half of the pinch bar is fastened to the wall; for maximum strength it should be anchored into the studs. If you cannot locate the studs, or if for some reason you find it impossible to fasten to them, the bar should be put up with toggle bolts or Molly bolts. It is quite important that the pinch bar is firmly anchored because leverage from the shelf can put a lot of pressure on it.

Assemble the shelf as shown in Figure 78. You can put a number of these up to make a system if you like, but keep the highest shelf below eye level for maximum hiding of the pinch bars. (See Figure 79.)

These shelves can be practically any length, but I recommend that the width be limited to 14 inches maximum. If you are making a long shelf, add 1 × 2 supports for the plywood every 24 inches or so. The supports become part of the framework and the plywood rests on top of them.

Because of the way it is attached to the wall, this is not a good system to use if children will be climbing on it—activity like that will tend to pull the pinch bar off the wall. Two great uses for this system would be as a serving counter in a dining room or as a telephone table; of course you will think of many other applications.

Figure 79

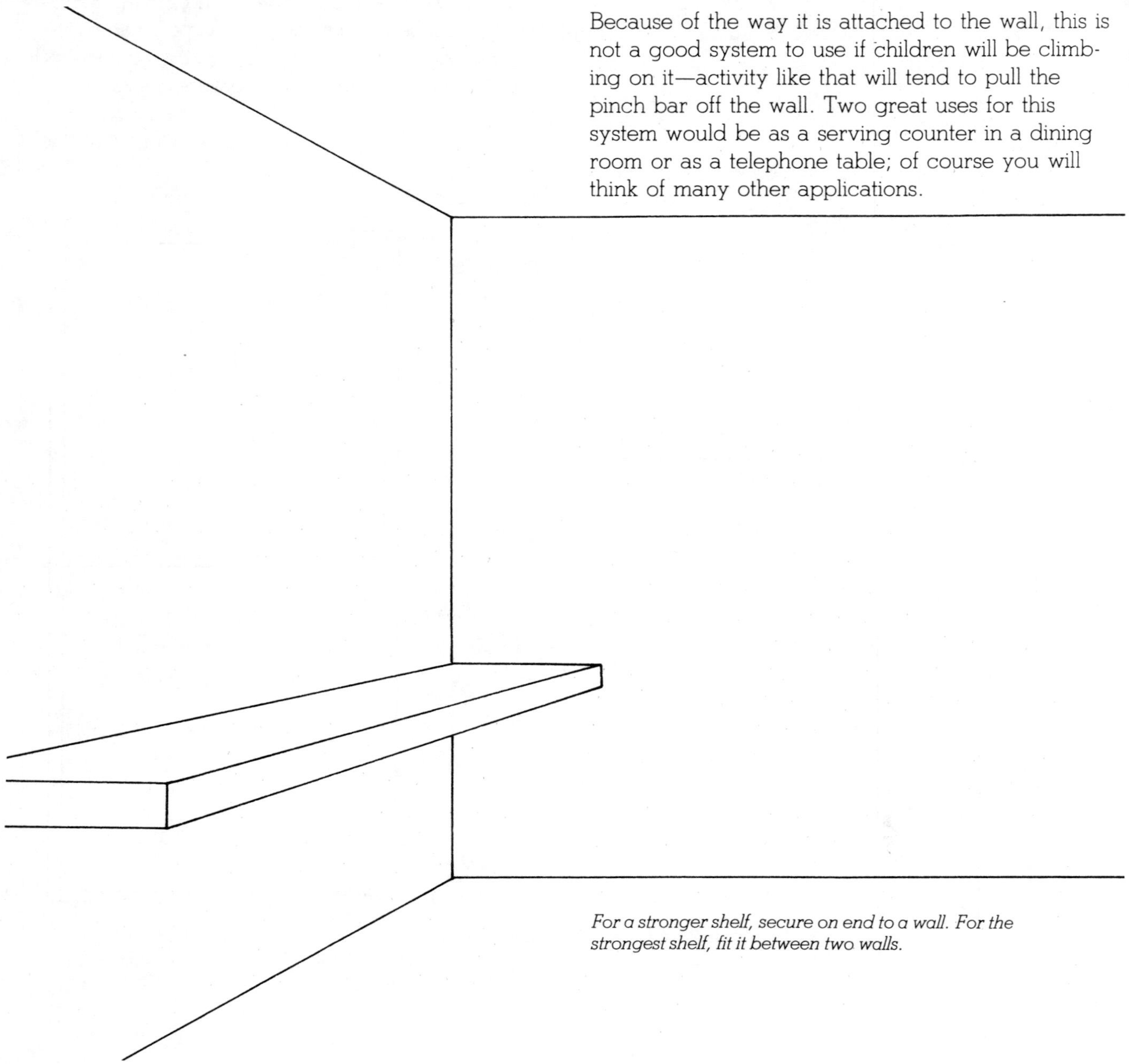

For a stronger shelf, secure on end to a wall. For the strongest shelf, fit it between two walls.

Pedestals

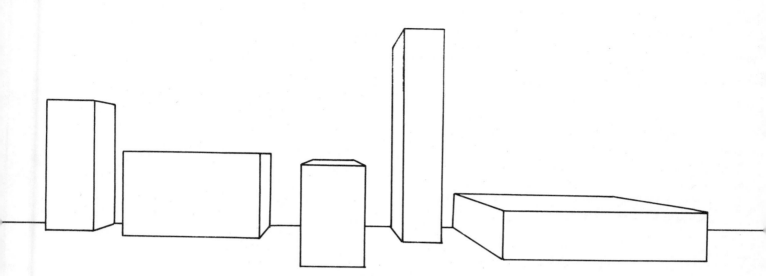

I've included pedestals in this part of the book because, although they are a bit of a departure from shelves per se, they are very useful for a wide variety of display purposes and they are easy to build.

A pedestal is really a five-sided rectangular box (no bottom is needed). Built using 3/4-inch plywood, a well constructed pedestal can hold almost anything from a fine piece of sculpture to heavy potted plants. They are great for holding TV sets and other electronic equipment, and are sure to add interest to any room.

The first step in building a pedestal is to decide, as always, how large the structure will be. Cut the four sides to the exact height that the final pedestal will be. The width of the sides will be the final width of the pedestal less 3/4 inch, because the sides overlap as shown in Figure 81. The four sides are assembled as shown and are nailed together using 1-1/4 inch finishing nails driven 1/8 inch below the surface of the wood. White glue is used in all joints. Fill all the nail holes with wood filler and sand them smooth.

The top piece is cut to fit exactly into the opening created by the four sides. To install the top, push it in place, turn the entire unit upside down, and nail.

Make certain that the top piece is all the way down at the floor before gluing and nailing.

The pedestal can be finished with any wood finish or paint. The plywood edges should be filled with wood filler and sanded before any finish is applied. Take the time to sand the unit well, particularly if you are planning to paint. Small seams that show can also be filled with wood filler; if well done, this will give the piece a solid feeling rather than the appearance of a number of pieces fastened together.

A grouping of these pedestals of different heights and widths can be a dazzling addition to any room.

Figure 81

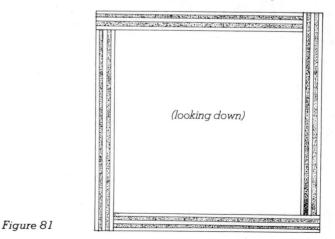

(looking down)

A KISS Shelf

My self-admonishing "Keep It Simple, Stupid" system strikes again. (See page 28.)

These shelves are very simple—three pieces of wood nailed or screwed together. But by expanding on the idea, or using a lot of these, a striking arrangement can be made.

They are made with 3/4-inch-thick pine boards, any width you like. Assembly is easy. Always glue the joints with white glue, regardless of whether you use nails or screws.

To hang them up, drill a hole near the top of each brace. A screw through this hole that goes into a plastic anchor in the wall holds them up. Correctly anchored, these small shelves can hold books, odds-and-ends, a telephone, you name it. I made one near my telephone to hold the phone books.

Consider using a whole bunch of these to make a wall of books. You can vary them in width and length to suit exactly what you are displaying or storing—and take them with you when you move. Mixing them with paintings, photographs, mirrors and plants can make a striking display.

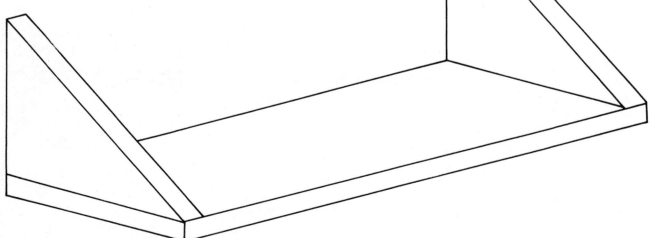

Figure 82

Part Four

Specialized Shelves

Bathroom Shelves

The bathroom always seemed to be the room short of storage space in my house. There are always two or three extra bottles or tubes of this or that lying around the tub or under the sink.

Here are two ideas that may help.

The first is simple. Look up the "Hanging Shelves" section in Part Three. Use nylon or another synthetic rope for hanging, and Plexiglass for the shelves proper. They are hung from the ceiling as before, or, for use in the shower, can be hung from the shower head or the like. Made with these materials, they are waterproof and easily cleaned. I added a mirror to my shower stall shelves and put my shaving cream and razor on the shelves. That way I can shave while I shower in the morning. This means less congestion in the bathroom and I really enjoy stepping out "all finished," as it were.

The second shelving idea for the bath is intended to go around the toilet. Before proceeding, however, two notes of caution are called for.

First, the water shut-off valve under the toilet should not be blocked from easy access. That valve can be very important in a plumbing emergency, so care should be taken to be sure you can get to it fast if needed.

The second warning concerns the tank itself. Sometimes, though not often, it is necessary to remove the top of the tank so that repairs to the workings

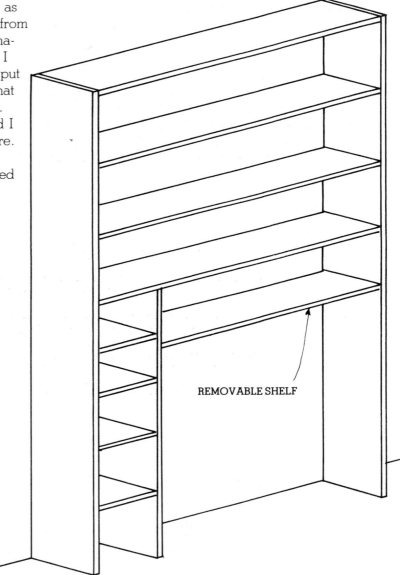

REMOVABLE SHELF

Figure 83

can be made. Therefore, make sure that you leave enough room between the tank top and the shelf closest to it so that the work can be done; or, make that shelf easily removable.

The shelves themselves can run from floor to ceiling or can be shorter if you desire. The shelves can be closed off with doors (see Part Five, "Things to Add" section), or they can be covered with a "flea market" framed mirror, my personal favorite.

The material for these shelves is "10-inch" pine (actually about 9-1/2 inches deep) or redwood. The one-inch thickness (actually 3/4 inch) will do nicely. Redwood is more resistant to moisture than pine; however, pine will hold up just as well if properly finished.

An average size for a toilet tank is about 9 inches deep by about 21 inches wide. Since the shelves should not protrude much beyond the tank depth, the 10-inch boards serve well. The width, of course, is determined by the space available and your own plans. If you make the shelves wider than the tank, a narrow column of shelves can extend to the floor that will easily hold odds-and-ends, an extra roll of paper, or a mini-library of paperback books.

The shelves are fastened together with *brass* wood screws. Screws are needed to hold the wooden unit together because of expansion and contraction resulting from the changes in moisture level in the room. Brass is specified to prevent rust.

The unit is assembled using the "butt joint" method as covered on page 57. The design you use can be similar to the one shown in Figure 83, or you can create your own.

Assemble the unit outside the bathroom, even if you must leave it a bit incomplete to allow you to fit it around the tank. Note that the bottom edges of the uprights may have to be notched out to clear the baseboard or tile base if there is one. Once the unit is assembled, it is carried in and stood in place.

If the unit is suitably stable, nothing further in the way of bracing is needed. If the unit is a bit shaky or you expect that children will be climbing on it, it is a good idea to secure it to the wall with small angle irons.

Finishing should be done with a water-repellent finish such as varnish or polyurethane for pine. Redwood is moisture-resistant and would not need to be finished at all, though it can be finished if you like.

TIP In finishing pine or redwood for bathroom use or other areas where there is a high moisture problem, be sure to coat both sides of the wood with finish. This will prevent the wood from absorbing moisture through the unfinished side and warping.

If you find or have a suitable framed mirror, attach it using a piece of "piano hinge." Piano hinge, available in hardware stores, is the kind of hinge that is continuous from the top to the bottom of the mirror. It is available in lengths from 12 inches to 6 feet; you may have to cut it with a hack saw to make it just the right size. (I recommend piano hinge because it will keep the door or mirror straight in spite of hard use.) A magnetic or friction cabinet catch, like the ones on a kitchen cabinet, completes the job.

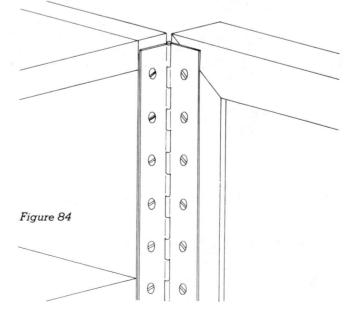

Figure 84

Lunch Counter/Bar (or Both)

Here is a neat design for a lunch counter, bar or both that is easy to build, attractive, and very functional. One side has shelves for all kinds of storage. The other side leaves space for people to sit up under the counter.

The counter/bar utilizes the standard 25-inch wide butcher-block counter top material available at most lumberyards. This butcher block comes in a variety of lengths, but for this example I will use the 5-foot-long size. These tops are not cheap, but they are made of solid rock maple and are nearly indestructible.

If the price of the butcher block exceeds your budget for the project, you can make your own "mock butcher block" out of 1 × 2 pine. Here's how to do it.

Assembling the pieces of 1 × 2 will make a top that is 24-3/4 inches wide rather than the 25 inches of the butcher block. This will not make any difference later on.

To make a 5 foot by 24-3/4 inch top, you will need 33 pieces of 1 × 2 that are 5 feet long. These are arranged side by side, glued with white glue and nailed as shown in Figure 86. When putting on the last piece, drive the nails below the surface of the wood with a nail set and fill the hole with a wood filler.

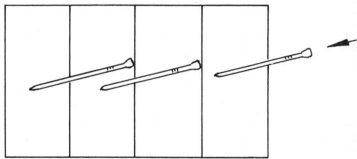

Figure 85

Once the top is assembled, sand the top until it is smooth and finish it with a good water- and alcohol-proof sealer such as varnish or polyurethane. Be sure to cover both sides of the top and all edges. So much for the mock butcher block top.

Figure 86

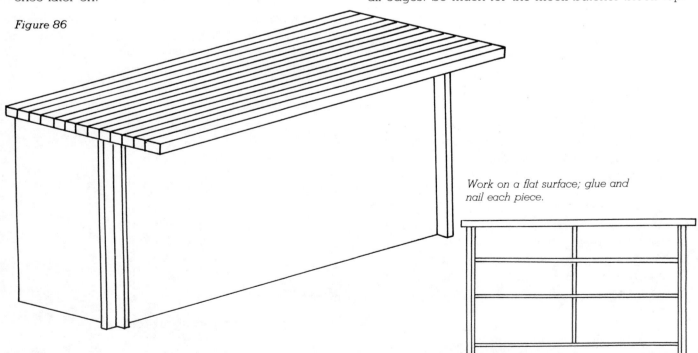

Work on a flat surface; glue and nail each piece.

The base that the counter top sits on can be made in any of several different heights: table height (30 inches), counter height (36 inches), or bar height (48 inches), depending on the use you have planned. The height you choose, less 1-1/2 inches (thickness of the top) will be the height of the uprights.

The upright structure is made from 3/4-inch plywood and consists of three pieces: two ends and a center divider. The unit is assembled using the "liquor box method" described in the "All Wood Shelves" section of Part Three.

The two ends are identical. Each is 20-3/4 inches wide; its height is 1-1/2 inches less than the total height as above. Figure 87 shows how it is cut. The dotted lines show how the cutting can be made more decorative and a suggested location for the slots that will eventually receive the shelves.

The center (lengthwise) divider is the same height as the end pieces and is 2 inches shorter than the length of the top. For a 5-foot top it would be 58 inches. The notches that receive the end pieces are 2 inches from the ends.

Inside the unit there are shelves. You can add as many shelves as you like and arrange them in any way to make the best storage area for your needs. The shelves are made of 10-inch wide pine or plywood.

If you will be storing heavy objects, a "middle-of-the-shelf" support will be needed. It is the same width as the shelves and will fit into notches in the shelves. It will not run all the way to the floor, but rather will sit on the bottom shelf. (See Figure 88.)

The reason that the middle-of-the-shelf support rests on the bottom shelf is that the bottom shelf is raised off the floor and a "kick plate" is installed under it.

Figure 87

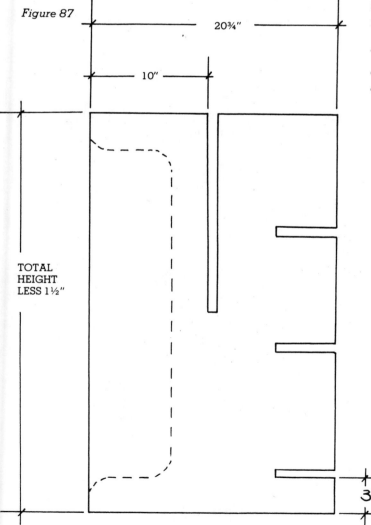

20¾"

10"

TOTAL
HEIGHT
LESS 1½"

3"

Figure 88

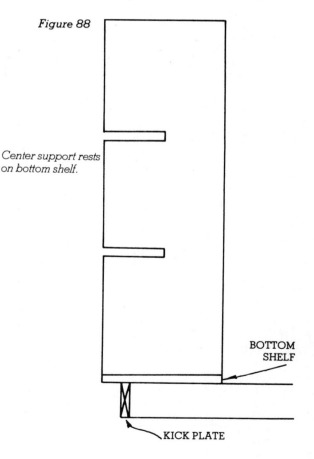

*Center support rests
on bottom shelf.*

BOTTOM
SHELF

KICK PLATE

This plate also prevents dirt from building up under the bottom shelf—a very hard place to clean.

The kick plate is made from a piece of 1 × 3 pine (3/4 × 2-1/2, actually). It is nailed between the two end supports at floor level; the bottom shelf rests on it. The kick plate is recessed 3 inches from the front edge of the shelf to allow for toe space.

To assemble the unit, slide the two ends onto the center divider. For a more permanent job, white glue can be added to the joints, although the unit will be stable enough without it. Next, nail the kick plate in place using 1-1/2-inch finishing nails. Drive the nails below the surface and fill the holes with wood filler. Next, install the bottom shelf.

Installing the top is the next step. It can be set on top and allowed to rest under its own weight, or it can be fastened in place. To secure the top, mark the line where the center divider meets the top, assuring that the top will be in the exact location you want it when the job is through. Remove the top and fasten a piece of 2 × 2 pine on the outside

of this line with wood screws. If you are using the maple butcher block, a pilot hole (hardwood size from the chart, Figure 14) is a must. Once the 2 × 2 is secured to the top, set the top back on the uprights and drive two screws through the center divider into the 2 × 2. The top is now secure. Note: place the 2 × 2 so that it will not interfere with the "center-of-the-shelves" support. (See Figure 89.)

Next, assemble the shelves and the center-of-the-shelves support and slide this assembly in place. I recommend that the complete unit be finished in some manner. Ideas for finishing are discussed in the "Planning and Design" section (Part One).

This unit makes a pleasant breakfast or lunch counter in a kitchen and adds lots of space for storing hard-to-store appliances like a blender, slow cooker, waffle iron, etc. Doors can be added to the shelves if desired.

This unit also makes a practical bar. Two or three stools can fit neatly in front with plenty of storage space for liquors and glassware behind. Consider adding a wine rack and a glass-storage shelf, as shown in the "Things to Add" Part of this book.

Figure 89

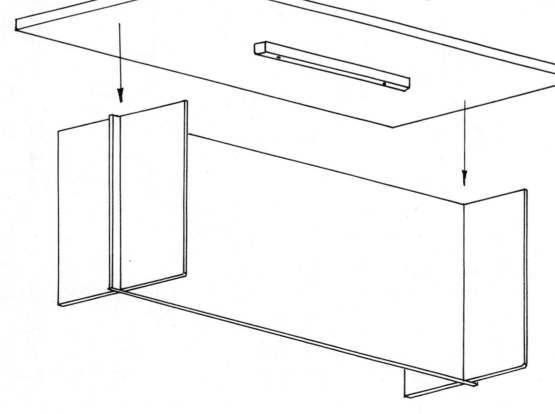

Over-the-Car Shelves

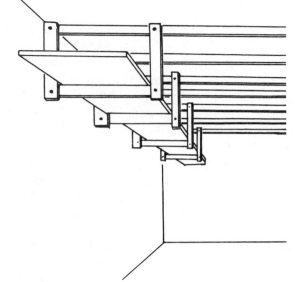

This shelf system adapts itself well to a wide variety of storage problems in a most difficult area to organize—the garage.

These shelves hang from the ceiling rafters (joists) in the usually wasted space above the hood or roof of the car. Since they will be in the garage, I will not pay too much attention to how they look; I'll give you the construction details, and you can fill in the decoration.

The shelf uprights are 1 × 4's or 2 × 4's that are bolted to the ceiling joists. The decision between the sizes of wood is made of the basis of weight. If you plan to store lightweight objects like window screens, etc., the 1 × 4's will be fine. If you plan to store heavier objects like garden products, newspapers, paints, etc., choose the 2 × 4's.

Each upright will bolt to the joist with two lag bolts. Choose a lag that will get at least one inch penetration into the joist. Depending on how large your shelf will be, you will need four or six uprights. Figure 90 shows how they are arranged.

The shelf supports that join the uprights and hold up the shelves are also 1 × 4's or 2 × 4's. They are lag bolted in place in the same manner as the uprights.

The bolts should be staggered, i.e., not placed one above the other nor placed side by side. A pilot hole will definitely be needed to prevent splitting.

The shelf is made from 3/4-inch exterior grade plywood. It is cut so that it fits snugly between the uprights and rests squarely on the shelf supports. It can be nailed in place if desired, but this is seldom necessary. For nailing, 1-1/2-inch finishing nails are fine.

TIP Once you have installed your over-the-car shelves, take a few extra minutes and install a car-stopper device to let the driver know when he or she has the car in proper place. The device is simply an old tennis ball suspended on a piece of string or light rope. It is hung so that it will just touch the base of the car's windshield when the car is far enough in the garage. Very simple and very effective.

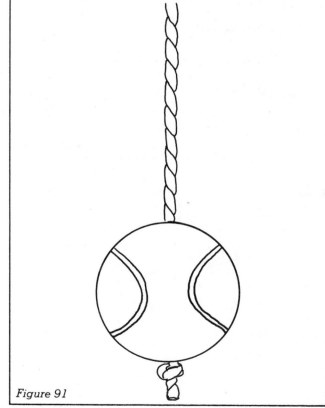

Figure 91

Under or Around the Stairs

Since there is a very wide variety of configurations for stairs, all sizes and shapes, this "specialized" section will by necessity be rather general. The spaces around and under stairs are often wasted; but with proper planning, a great volume of storage space can be gained, often with an improvement in appearance.

UNDER STAIRS

For clarity, let us begin by defining two terms. The *tread* is the part of the stairs you step on. The *riser* is the vertical section of the stairs that forms the back between each tread.

The upright of one end of the under-stairs shelves will be the risers. The other will be built by you or whomever you can talk into doing the work for you. The heights of the shelves will be determined by the location of each riser.

Each shelf rests on a piece of molding (1/2-inch quarter-round works well) which is nailed or screwed into the riser.

A difficulty can arise if, as is often the case, the risers are made from hardwood. If this is the case, drill a pilot hole through the molding and into the riser. The size of the drill to be used is found on the pilot hole chart (Figure 14). After the holes are drilled, use wood screws to fasten the molding in place.

Since most stairways are wider by far than most ordinary sets of shelves, you may want to make these shelves extra deep to take advantage of all that space. Extra-wide shelves can be made from a large sheet of plywood; or you can make them by using two or more pieces of shelving pine, side by side.

Figure 92

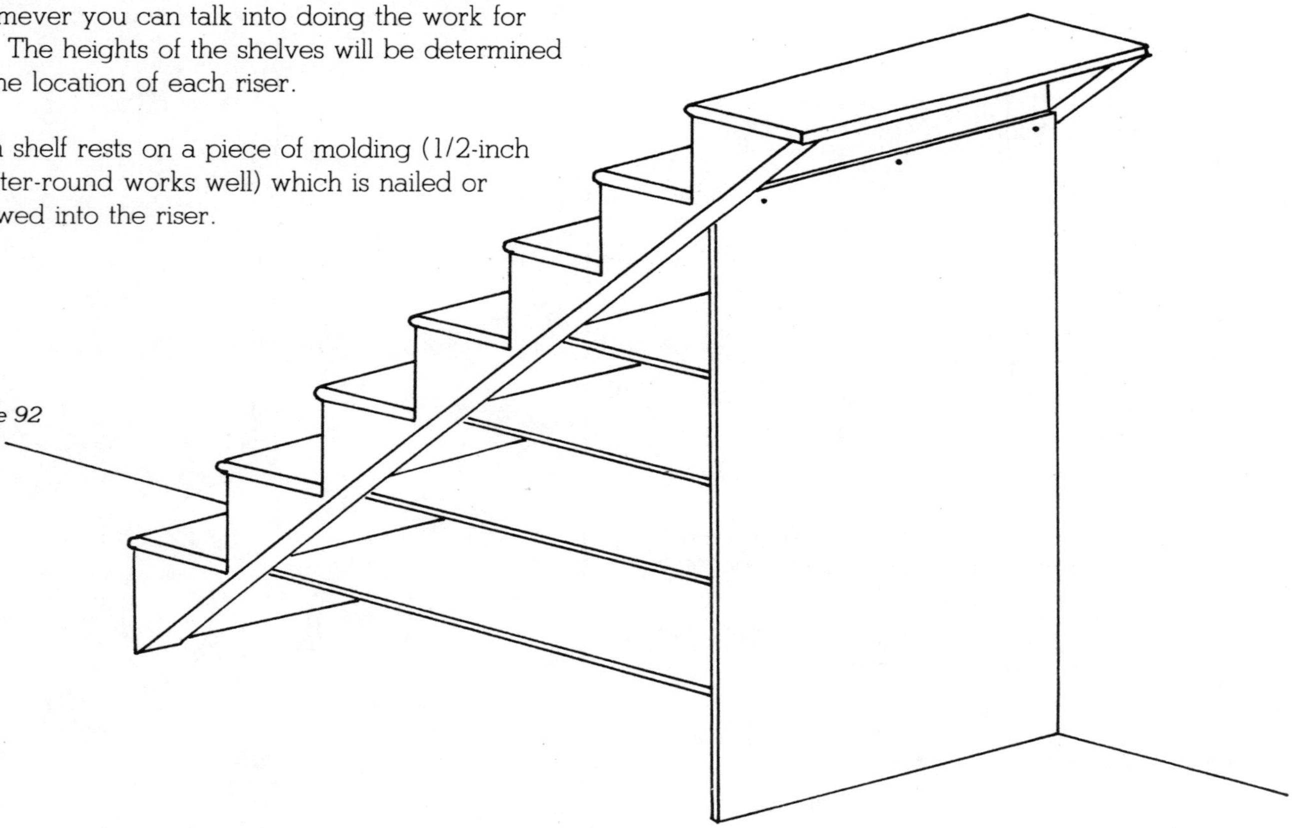

The upright you build is fastened to the highest riser. Once it is cut and its size is checked, it is laid down on the floor. Next measure the height of each shelf support that you installed on the risers. Transfer the measurements to the support on the floor. Mark a line across the upright at that distance. Fasten a piece of molding just below the line; the shelf will rest on this molding just as it rests on the molding you fastened to the riser. If you have measured accurately, the shelves will be level.

Stand the upright you made in place and fasten it to the top riser with wood screws. Again, pilot holes will be needed if the riser is hardwood. Now cut and install the shelves. This step is saved for last so that the length of each shelf (each will be different) can be accurately measured. The shelves are then each cut to the correct length.

The upright you made will need to be secured at the bottom as well as at the top. Driving a few finishing nails into the shelf through the upright will handle the job easily.

TIP Here is a method for fastening two or more pieces of shelving pine together to make wider boards. The boards are laid side by side on the floor and corrugated fasteners join them together. Once the boards are aligned, the fasteners are driven with a special tool so that they span the joints of the boards. This will make a most satisfactory joint.

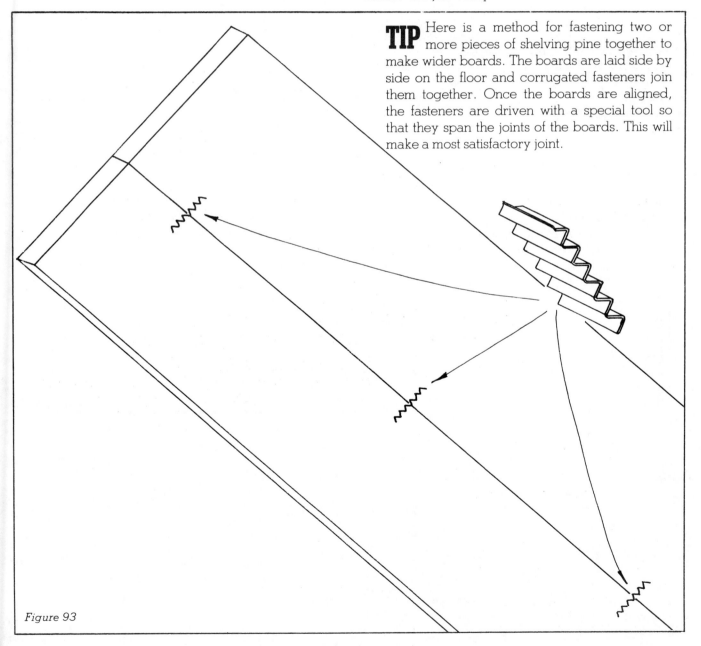

Figure 93

IN THE BEND

If you have stairs that take a turn, the floor space next to the stairs can be a very attractive location for a set of shelves.

The construction for shelves in this area is the same as for other free-standing shelf systems covered earlier. A unit that has a back will create a "wall" of shelves next to the stairs. A backless unit will create more storage without disturbing the openness too much.

Such a unit filled with plants, books, etc. can be a really attractive addition to the decor to a hallway.

Figure 94

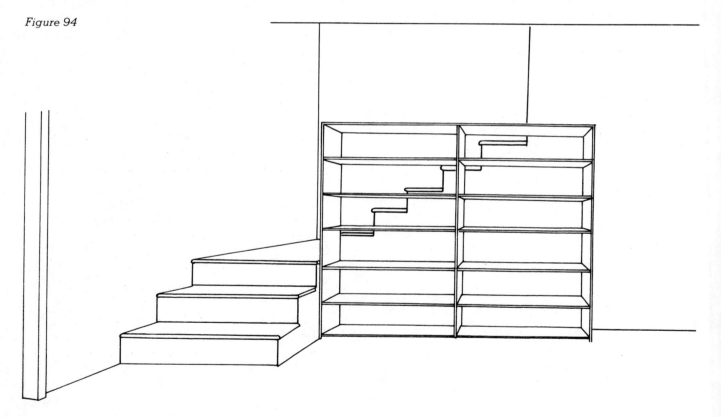

Revolving Shelves

Did you ever have a closet or other space that you wanted to utilize for storage but discover that the use of ordinary shelves was far from ideal? Here is a set of shelves that will allow you to reach the items on the back of the shelves without having to reach over the ones in front. This system, although a bit more complicated to build than some of the others, can be supremely useful and convenient. (See Figure 95.)

In essence, these revolving shelves are a multi-layered lazy Susan. All the shelves turn as a unit.

The upright for the revolving shelves is a center pole made of metal pipe. Steel or iron is the most suitable material for the pipe; copper and plastics are too flexible.

The outer diameter of the pipe can be between 3/4 inch and 1-1/2 inches, depending on the weight of

objects the shelves are to hold. Choose a "stock-size" pipe, however, to make sure you can easily get the other hardware you'll need to complete the job. Stock sizes are 3/4 inch, 1 inch, and 1-1/2 inches.

The pipe upright is secured at the top and the bottom in a flange that allows it to spin but prevents it from falling to the right or left. The flange is fastened to the floor and to the upper support with wood screws. Remember that flooring is usually hardwood, so pilot holes (see chart, Figure 14) will be needed.

For very heavy loads or for smoother rotation, a ball bearing is added between the end of the pipe and the floor inside the lower flange. I recommend using the bearing if you can find one. Check the listing for "bearings" in your Yellow Pages for a starting point. If the dealers listed there do not sell

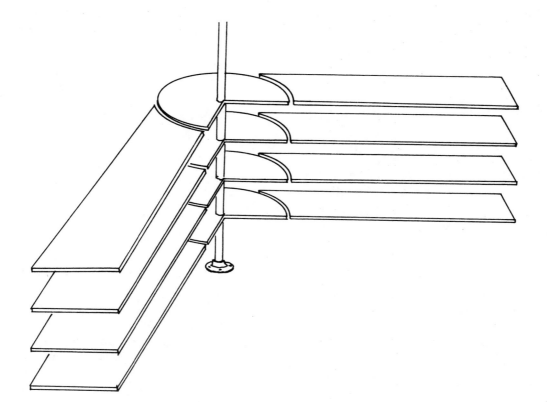

Figure 95

to the public (the problem I had), ask that he or she suggest a retail outlet where you can purchase or order the bearing that you want.

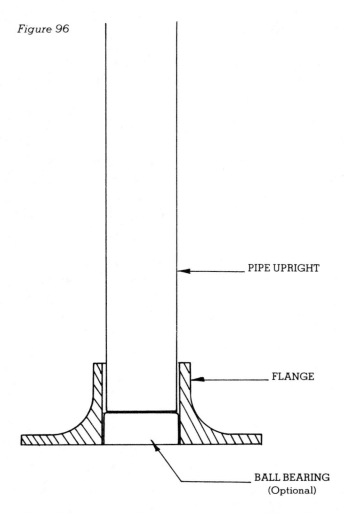

Figure 96

PIPE UPRIGHT

FLANGE

BALL BEARING
(Optional)

The shelves themselves are made from 3/4-inch plywood. They can be cut so they are 1/4, 1/2, 3/4, or all of a full circle. The 1/4-circle shelves make neat little "swing outs." The 1/2-circle shelves can be incorporated into any straight set of shelves or used where minimal intrusion into the adjoining area is required. The 3/4-circle shelves make a neat corner section where two other sets of shelves meet at a right angle. The full-circle shelves will of course give the most shelf area. (See Figure 97.)

Laying out the shelves is done with a home-made compass made from a nail or tack, a piece of string and a pencil. Once you have decided how wide you want your shelves, here is how to lay them out.

First, determine where you want the center of the circle (from which all the shelf variations are made) to be. Drive the tack or nail there. Tie the string to the nail, leaving 6 inches or more than you will need. Subtract 1/4 inch so that there is a little extra space for the shelves to swing or rotate smoothly. I selected 1/4 inch arbitrarily; you can increase or decrease it depending on your needs. The width of the shelf less the 1/4 inch will be the distance from the nail to the pencil point. Tie the string to the pencil and push the string down as close to the pencil point as possible. Recheck your measurement. Leave the extra string on; you will need it later. Now, keeping the string taut, draw your way around the circle.

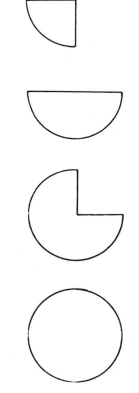

Figure 97

If you will be using less than the full circle, you will now have to divide the newly drawn circle into parts. All of the divisions will be based on a nice, straight line drawn across the diameter of the circle. This line will pass through the center of the circle where the nail or tack is, so remove it before drawing the line. You now have the cutting line for the 1/2-circle shelves.

For 1/4- or 3/4-circle shelves, you will need another diameter drawn at exactly 90 degrees (a right angle) to the first. This line will also pass through the nail or tack hole. If you have a reliable square, just lay it on the first line and make the new diameter. If you don't have a reliable square, proceed as follows to draw a 90-degree (right) angle using only a compass and a straightedge.

This is a trick my geometry teacher taught me way back in high school. It is easy and extremely accurate. Here's how to do it using the tack, string, and pencil we used for marking the circle as the compass (see Fig. 98):

(1) Push the tack or nail in where the diameter crosses the outside edge of the circle. (point "A").

(2) Make the string at least 3 inches longer than it was to draw the circle. The exact length is not critical; keeping the same length for the other side will be important.

(3) Draw an arc as shown (Arc One).

(4) Move the tack, string, and pencil, and push the tack in at point B.

(5) Draw Arc Two.

(6) From the point where Arc One crosses Arc Two (marked "D" on the drawing), draw a straight line through the center of the circle (marked point "C") and continue this line until it makes a complete diameter.

That's all there is to it, you have made the 90 degree (right) angle.

You will find that it will be easier to drill the holes needed now, before the shelves are actually cut. In each shelf you will need to cut a hole that is the same size or slightly larger than the pipe upright. A butterfly bit or a hole cutter is the correct tool for making holes 3/4 inch or larger.

Each shelf is fastened to the pole upright using a flange that is similar to, or exactly the same as, the ones used to hold the top and bottom of the pipe. The flange is screwed to the shelf and is then bolted to the pipe. Sometimes you can find flanges that have set screws (small screws built in for holding the flange tightly to a pipe). If you find these, use them. They will be easier to use than the drilling required for the others.

Figure 98

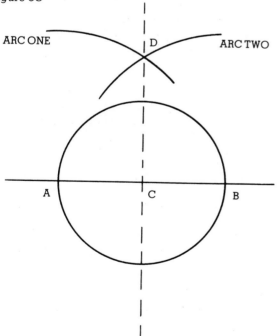

ARC ONE   D   ARC TWO

A   C   B

Figure 99

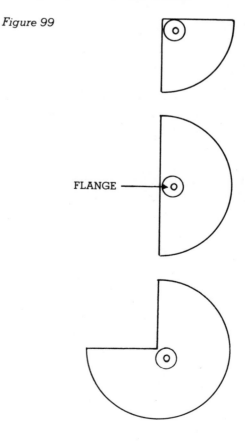

FLANGE

Correctly locating the hole will depend upon the shape of the shelf you are using. If you are using a full-circle shelf, the hole will be drilled exactly in the middle of the shelf. For all the other shapes, take the flange and place it on the uncut board. Locate it as close to the edge or corner as possible without allowing the flange to extend past the edge. In other words, the flange should be completely on the wood shelf, as close to its pivot point as possible (see Figure 99). With the flange in place, draw a line around the inside of the flange (where the pipe will fit); this will be the location of the hole.

TIP A useful tip for drilling such large holes in plywood is *not* to drill all the way through from one side. Doing so has the danger of splitting some of the wood away as the drill bit exits. To avoid this, drill through from one side until the small point of the bit comes through the other side. Then flip the board over, place the small point of the bit in the hole left from the first drilling, and complete the hole from the new side. This will eliminate any chipping or splitting, since the drill never exits.

Now is the time, with all holes drilled, to cut the shelves out. A sabre saw will give the easiest way. After cutting, some sanding of the edges will be needed.

Each shelf is fastened to a flange as mentioned earlier, and each flange-and-shelf assembly is bolted to the pipe upright. Once the holes are drilled, the flange is screwed to the shelf. Use the pipe to get the proper alignment if needed.

A trial fitting is recommended at this point. Before drilling the holes through the flanges and upright (or tightening the set screws if you have the set-screw type), set the complete unit up in place where it will be located and check for any problems such as clearances, etc. Once you are satisfied that all is well, determine the exact height of the shelves and, holding the pipe in a vise if possible, drill the hole for the bolt.

Once all the holes are drilled for all the shelves, bolt the flange-and-shelf assemblies to the upright. You are now ready for the final installation.

Stand the pipe-and-shelves assembly in the approximate spot where it will finally be located. Move the pipe around a bit until you find the exact spot where the shelves spin freely and fit as you intended. Mark this spot on the floor with a pencil by drawing around the outside of the pipe.

Take the flange you are using for the floor and (inserting the ball bearing if you are using one) line it up with the pencil mark in the floor. Drill the pilot holes and screw it in place.

Next, slip the upper flange over the top of the pipe and stand the whole assembly in the flange on the floor. Now slide the upper flange up to the top support and, making sure everything moves freely, mark its location. Install the screws for the top flange and the job is done.

The edges of the shelves can be sanded and filled with wood filler, if you like, or you can nail an aluminum edge molding around them. The system can be painted or finished with any of the finishes covered in the "Planning and Design" section.

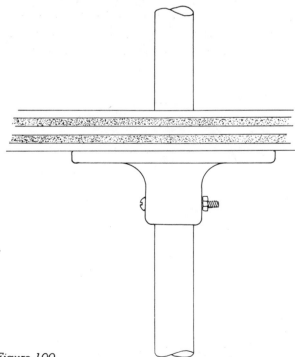

Figure 100

Part Five
Things To Add

Cubby Holes

Here is a handy addition of any shelf system, a lot of little places to put a lot of little things. And by the way, you don't have to use these just on shelves. How about on your desk or workbench; hang the unit on a wall to display knick-knacks, or to use for mail or newspapers. I once used one of these for messages where every person in the house (or office) had one little box of his or her own. The message was just slipped in the box. If the person didn't find it, it was his own fault, everyone knew where to look for messages.

A quick way to get a lot of little cubbies is to find one of the wooden cases that soft drinks come in—24 quick cubby holes and no work. Since these are becoming somewhat scarce, they're becoming camp, too.

Want something a little fancier or something built to your exact specifications? OK, here is a plan that mixes the liquor box method and butt joints to make a set of cubby holes of any size or shape you want.

Make a quick sketch of the cubby holes you want. The only limit to the dimensions is what will fit in the shelves.

Figure 101

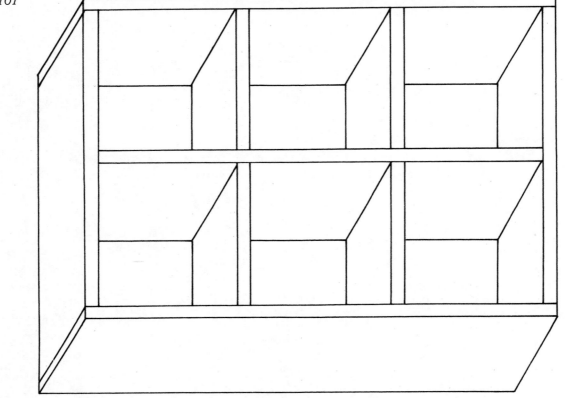

The complete unit may be made from any kind of 1/4-inch wood. Plexiglass (1/4 inch) can also be used.

The interior dividers are cut and assembled using the liquor box method (described in the "All Wood Shelves" section). Once the interior dividers are complete, assemble them. The unit can be used just as is or the outside pieces can be added.

If you want the outside pieces, measure how large they will need to be and cut the wood or plexi to size. The illustration (Figure 101) shows how they fit together.

Fasten wood pieces together using white glue and small brads (3/4 inch is a good size). Allow the glue to dry at least 12 hours before putting any stress on the unit. The nails are small enough that they probably will not need to be driven below the surface. If they are shiny, touch them on top with a brown or black felt tip pen.

If your outsides are Plexiglass, assemble them with plexi solvent or cement. Put on one side at a time and hold it in place with rubber bands until the solvent or cement is dry. Then install the next piece and so on.

The wood cubby holes can be finished to match the shelves or can be colored for contrast, if you like.

If you want to hang a set of these on the wall, add two small blocks of wood, screwed to the inside of the top where it will meet the wall. These blocks are then screwed into the wall or into plastic anchors.

Glassware Holders

If you have a set or an assortment of glassware
with stems, here is an idea for a shelf to hold them,
ready for use and, depending on where the shelf is
located, an addition to the decor of your room.

The glasses hang upside down, the stems fitting into
slots in the shelf. The spacing between the slots is
determined by the size of the individual glasses.
The slots are cut as deeply as possible, but leaving
no less than 2-1/2 inches along the back edge.

One of these shelves in or near the counter/bar unit
makes a convenient addition. Glassware is less
likely to break when it is stored in this way.

If you have non-stem glasses, they can be stored in
the diagonal boxes described in the "Wine Racks"
section. The boxes are made smaller, about 3 inches or whatever size is best for the glasses you are
storing. Six inches deep is usually adequate except
for tall beer glasses.

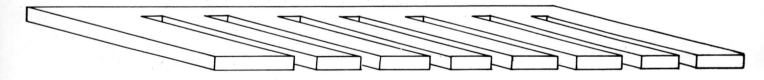

Figure 102   The size and spacing of slots can be varied for specific glasses.

Record Holders

According to the people who are supposed to know about such things, the correct way to store records to minimize warping is with the records standing upright. Here we'll cover ways to accomplish this.

The easiest way to add a record holder to your shelves is to buy one. There are many different sizes and styles available. These work well, but I suggest fastening them down to the shelves if possible, thus ensuring that the complete rack cannot inadvertently be pulled off the shelf. Aesthetically, however, they usually leave a lot to be desired.

I know of one type of purchased record holder that is not very objectionable in appearance, that is easy to install and works well. It consists of a number of poles that are held up between the shelves by internal tension created by a spring. You will need at least two; you can use them to divide your records into categories, if you like.

But, since you've put time and work into building your shelves, why not invest a little more time and make your own record storage system, tailored exactly to your needs?

A record album cover is exactly 12 inches square (check your collection for an odd-ball). Here are a few ideas for use with shelves that are 12 inches deep or deeper. (If you have shelves that are less than 12 inches deep, hang on—there will be one for you, too.)

Here's an easy method. Cut small blocks of wood about 1/4 inch wide, 1/2 inch high, and 10 inches long. Glue these blocks along the 1/4-inch edge every 6 inches or so along the bottom shelf and directly above on the upper shelf (Figure 103). A good epoxy or white glue will hold them in place. If your shelves are too far apart to use the little blocks, just increase the 1/2-inch dimension on the block until the upper block overlaps the record by

1/2 inch or so. Paint or finish the blocks to match the rest of the shelf.

Another method, which is just a variation of the preceding, uses a sheet of 1/4-inch wood rather than the blocks. The wood sheet is cut to be snug between the shelves and about 10 inches deep. It is installed with glue, as before, and is recessed about 2 inches from the front of the edge of any record so that there is room to grab hold of the record (see Figure 103A). Finish to match the shelf.

Figure 103

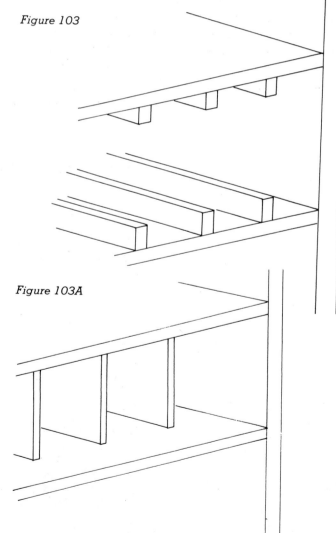

Figure 103A

A third method is to substitute 1/4-inch dowels for the wood dividers. You will need two pieces of dowel in place of each wood sheet. The dowels are located along the line where the wood divider would have been, and are placed about 2 inches from the back edge and 2 inches in from where the front of the record will fall. (See Figure 104.)

The dowels are fit into 1/4-inch holes drilled part

Figure 104

way through the shelf. If you wish the assembled rack to be permanent, put a drop or two of white glue in each hole before installing the dowel. To assemble, install all of the dowels in the lower holes after removing the upper shelf. Then replace the upper shelf and push the dowels around until they all fall into their corresponding holes on the under-side of the upper shelf.

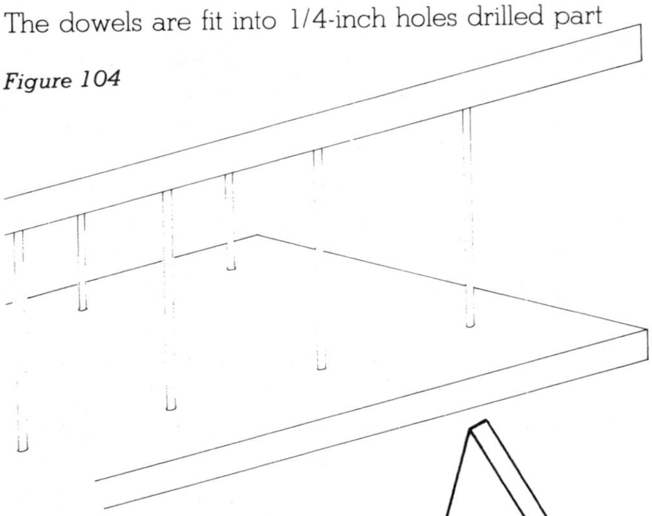

The dowels can be finished to match the rest of the shelf or can be colored to contrast if you like.

OK, now to the shelves that are less than 12 inches deep.

The answer to this storage situation is to store the records at an angle. A way to figure out the angle without resorting to the high school math we have all forgotten is simply to stand a record on the shelf and move it about until one corner sits on the front edge of the shelf without overlapping, and one corner sits on the back edge of the shelf without overlapping and the record is standing straight up. Mark this angle with a pencil and you have it. (See Figure 105.)

Any of the three methods described above can be used when the blocks, sheets, or dowels are installed along the angled lines.

Arrange your dividers so that there are between 12 and 20 records between dividers.

Figure 105

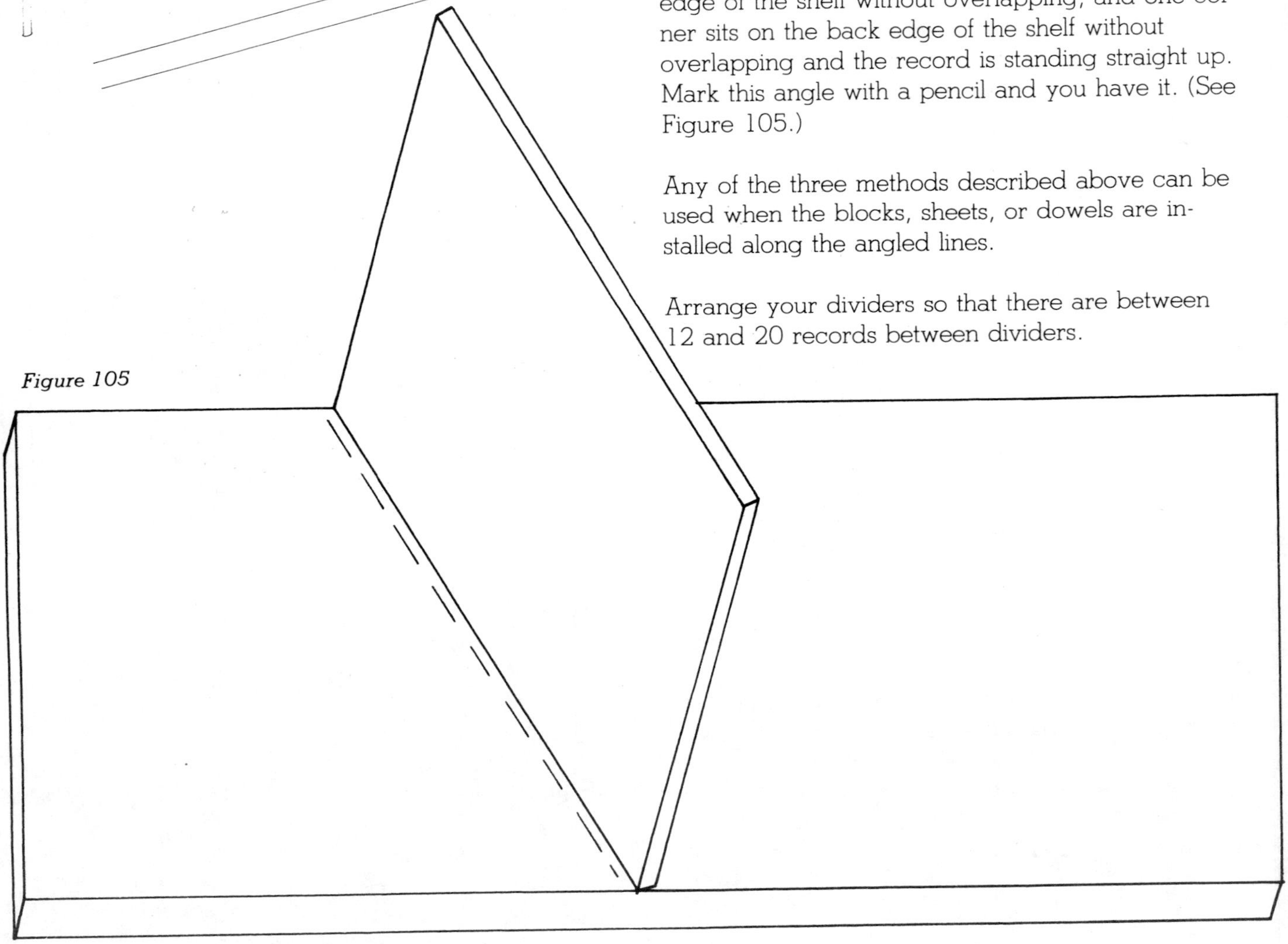

Wine Racks

Wines, specifically, those sealed with a cork, are best stored on their side. This, according to the experts, keeps the cork moist and hence tight in the neck of the bottle, thus blocking the intrusion of air into the bottle and retarding spoiling. Also, a moist cork holds together better when a corkscrew is used to remove it so that small bits of cork are kept out of the wine.

Aside from these practical advantages, bottles of wine stored in an attractive wine rack are an addition to the decor of a room.

There is a wide variety of wine racks you can buy that will fit nicely in shelves. Import stores and department stores are fruitful sources.

However, if you would like to make your own, or custom make one to your specific needs, here are a few ideas that may help.

An easy method for making a wine rack is to cut 12-inch pieces of cardboard mailing tubes, about 4 inches in diameter. These can be purchased in a well stocked stationery store or art store. (See Figure 106.)

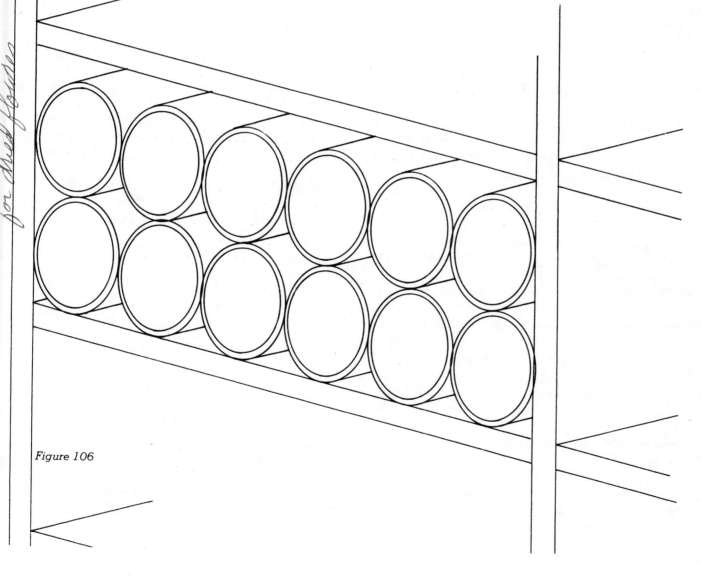

Figure 106

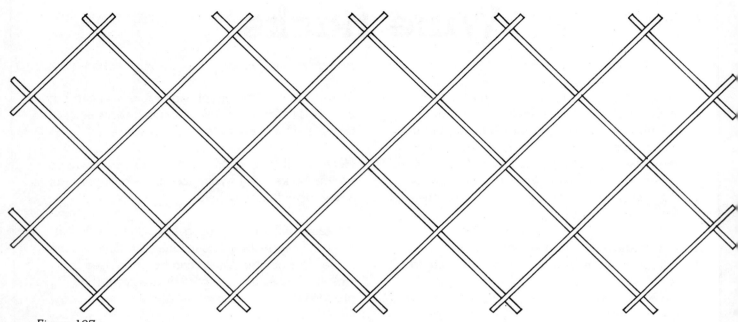

Figure 107

The tubes are arranged between the shelves so that the entire space from one upright to the next is filled; hence the tubes need no extra support.

If you want your tube wine rack to be smaller than the complete shelf width and height, the rack can be made to be freestanding by putting two bands of fiber-glass strapping tape around it.

Either way, paint the unit with spray paint.

There is a more conventional type of wine rack that I call diagonal boxes. It is made completely from 1/4-inch wood (pine, plywood, or hardwood) or from Plexiglas. A rack large enough to hold 14 bottles will fit in a space 30 inches wide, 13 inches high and 12 inches deep. (See Figure 107.)

The rack is made from pieces of wood or plexi 12 inches wide cut 6 inches deep (4 pieces needed), 14 inches deep (4 pieces needed), and 18 inches deep (6 pieces needed). Notches are cut into them so that they can fit together in the good old liquor box method (described in the "All Wood Shelves" section).

If you would like to make a unit of different size from the one shown, here is a simple way to calculate the length of the pieces: 4 inches per box along its length plus 2 inches for the overlap (1 inch each end). To locate the notches, measure in 1 inch from one end and center a notch there. The balance of the notches are centered every 4 inches thereafter. To center the notch, make a line at the measured distance and measure 1/8 inch on either side of the line.

The 1/8-inch-wide notches are cut into one-half the width of the board (6 inches in the case of a 12-inch-wide board). The distance of one-half the width will be constant, regardless of the width you make a wine rack.

The pieces are assembled as shown in Figure 107. A rack made of wood can be stained or painted. Greater interest might be created by staining or painting the pieces different colors before the rack is assembled.

If the rack is made from Plexiglass, you can choose clear, smoked, or any of a wide assortment of colors. These can also be mixed if you like.

Another variation of the same system can be made using rope instead of wood or plexi. This is done by drilling holes in the upper and lower shelves at both the front and back as shown in Figure 108.

The ropes are made of two vertical pieces knotted on each end and one long piece which is weaved through the rest of the holes. The vertical pieces are installed first. Take care to get them as tight as possible. Then weave the long rope, making it as tight as you can. It will need a knot on each end.

Special attention must be paid to the points where the ropes cross, as these will need to be reinforced or fastened together in some fashion. Following are two suggestions you can use. (If you have a better way, a fancy way of knots or something, by all means use it.)

The first suggestion uses fiber-glass strapping tape to hold the joint tight. Make one loop going horizontally and one vertically. When this is done, take some brown twine or string and wrap the entire joint until the tape is covered. The string wrapping is for appearance only. (See Figure 109.)

The second method is to push a small nail through both ropes at the point of intersection. It is a good idea to wrap those joints with twine also, to prevent the pin or nail from working itself out.

Give special attention to the points where the rope wraps around the vertical pieces. Either of the above methods are adequate, but take some extra care.

If you have appropriately placed uprights, the vertical ropes can be eliminated and the long woven rope can be passed through holes drilled in the uprights.

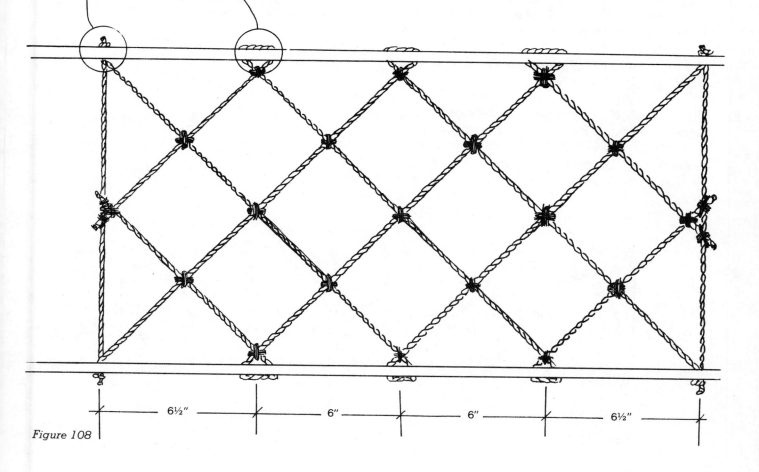

Figure 108

Another simple wood rack for storing a single layer of wine bottles is made by using two straight pieces of wood or plexi with 3-1/2- or 4-inch holes cut in them. The holes for the wood piece can be marked by tracing around the outside of a one-pound coffee can. Marking the plexi can be a little tricky, so try the following method, which has worked for me many times.

Using the same one-pound coffee can, trace around its outside with a sharp scriber, an ice pick, or a sharp nail. Use enough pressure to make a visible scratch. Then take a grease pencil (also called a china marker) and fill the scratch in with the pencil material. Rub any excess grease away from the scratch line and you will find that you now have an easily visible line.

For either wood or plexi, drill a hole 1/4 inch or larger inside the circumference of the circle you have drawn. A sabre saw or coping saw is inserted into the hole and the rest of the circle is cut out. On plexi, you may want to put a couple of pieces of masking tape on the sole plate of the saw to prevent it from scratching the plexi.

Make several of these holes across the board, leaving at least 1/2 inch between holes.

The front and back pieces (the back piece is optional) are fastened between the uprights using two small blocks of wood. The wood block is fastened to the upright and the piece of wood or plexi is fastened to the block with small screws.

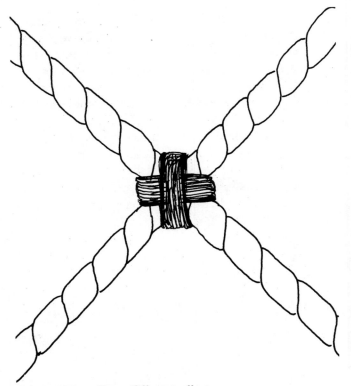

Figure 109   For a different effect, wrap the junction with brass wire.

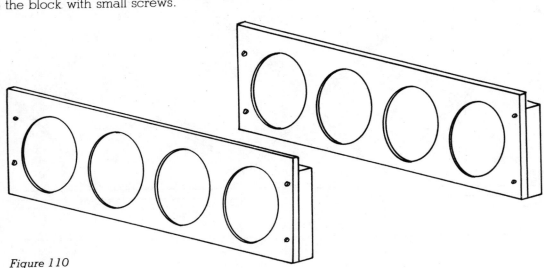

Figure 110

Special Trim

This section will show ways to add decorative and functional trim to shelf units. Although most of the ideas shown in the figures apply to the build-it-yourself shelves covered earlier in the book, many can be used with the units made from store-bought hardware as well. So take a look through them and see if there are some you can use.

I'll describe the various stages of adding special trim in an order that I hope may allow you to add the pieces you want one at a time, yet still have a neatly finished piece at each stage, even if you plan to add more pieces. If you work around the house like I do, there will be a real advantage. I tend to do the bulk of the work all at one time, and then do the final details over the period of the next few weeks on a catch-as-catch-can basis.

ADDING SIDES

Sides can be added to almost any shelf system that doesn't have them already as part of its uprights. The sides are made from pieces of wood—solid or plywood—that are the same width as the shelves.

The sides can be any height you want and can run from the floor to the ceiling. If you want to keep movable shelves within the sides, they must not be nailed to the shelves for support. Fasten the sides to the floor and the ceiling (or the top shelf) using wood blocks.

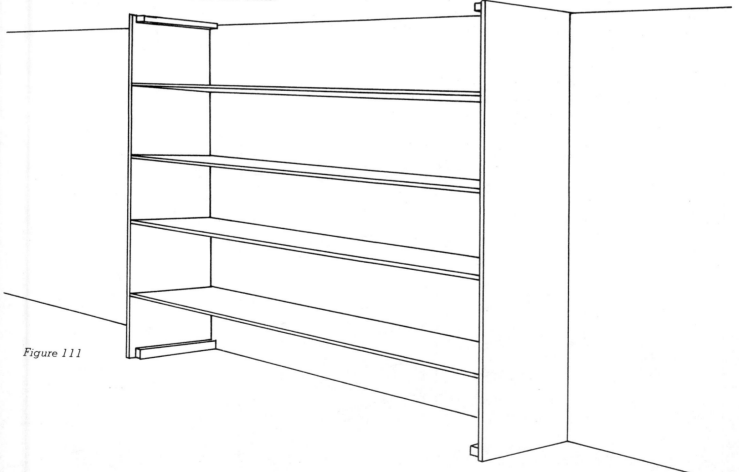

Figure 111

The blocks are first fastened to the wall or ceiling (make sure they get into the studs or are otherwise securely held), or screwed into the floor and the sides are screwed into them. Do not nail the sides to the blocks, as the force of striking the nails will in all likelihood loosen the blocks.

Once the sides are in place and secure, the unit can be left as is or front trim can be added.

FRONT TRIM

The purpose of front trim is to make the shelves seem like more of a unit, neater, and more decorative. This trim can also add to the strength of the unit and creates fastening points for doors and other additions covered later in this part of the book.

The trim is made from "one by" pine; the width is determined by taste. One-by-two is adequate, while one-by-three gives a more solid or heavy look. Figure 112 shows what this trim looks like and how it is arranged. There are, of course, many other variations that you can use.

Kick plate

The bottom-most piece between the sides is called the kick plate. The kick plate is recessed about 3 inches from the front of the shelves so that you can stand right up to them and have a space for your toes. If, however, your lowest shelf is high enough off the floor so that your feet can easily fit under (and the space is large enough to make cleaning easy), the kick plate can be left off. In my experience, though, the kick plate adds to the built-in feeling of the shelves; if the kick plate is left off, there may be the feeling that something is missing.

Figure 112

KICK PLATE

The kick plate is made from a piece of 1 × 3 and is nailed in place using 1-1/4-inch finishing nails. It is nailed to the sides and through the lowest shelf; the nails are driven in 1/8 inch below the surface and the holes left are filled with wood filler. The kick plate is often painted black to mask marks from shoes, but can be finished to match the rest of the shelves, of course. It should be finished in some way, since dirt will in time become imbedded in the wood and make it unsightly if it is not coated.

Edge boards

Edge boards are phase two of front trim. They are 1 × 2's or 1 × 3's added to the edges of the sides and centered on the uprights. These can also be added where there is no upright to give the impression of divided spaces.

Note: if you will be using top boards, as described below, you will want to wait to install the edges; it is useful to add them to the top boards and make a frame.

The edge boards are nailed to the sides and to the uprights using 1-1/4-inch finishing nails, and, as before, the nails are driven about 1/8 inch below the surface and the holes left are filled with wood filler and sanded smooth. These edge boards can also be added to the edges of the shelves if you want to make the shelves look thicker; and, if nailed raised up a bit, the edge boards will make a lip for the shelves as well. To keep the shelves movable, do not secure the edge boards on the shelves to the sides.

Top boards

Top Boards, with or without being jazzed up (discussed a little later), give a shelf system a feel of solidness and unity with the room. They also enhance the built-in look so that the shelves don't really look like they have been added to the room.

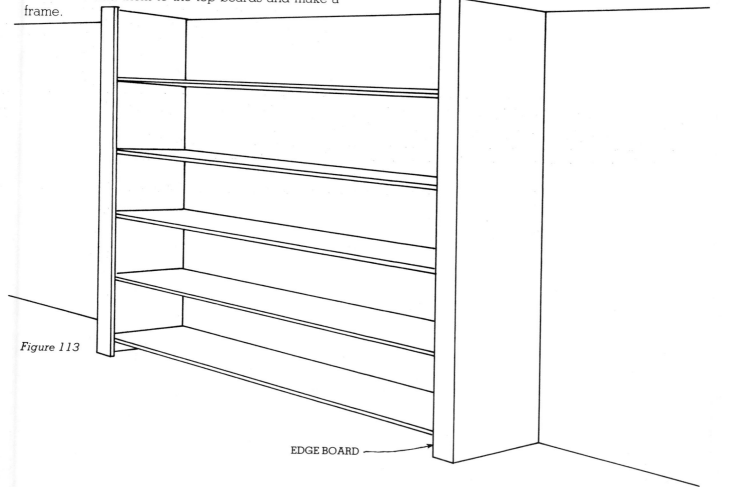

Figure 113

EDGE BOARD

The first step in making the top board is to decide how wide it will be. It can be any width from about 4 inches to 10 inches and even wider in some applications. Remember, however, that the wider the top board is, the more you lose access to the top shelf.

The top board is cut to the full width of the shelf unit less the width of the two outside edge pieces (it fits inside these). The top board will be joined to the two outside edge boards and then will be installed as a unit, making a sort of framework. The framework will be nailed into the sides and screwed into a block on the ceiling, much the same as the way the sides were fastened.

The top-board and edge-board framework is assembled using corrugated nails and the special tool for driving them. The nails are driven so that they span the joints where the boards meet, hence

holding them together. However, the fasteners are not adequate for holding the frame together permanently; hence the need for nails and screws.

Adding fancy cuts or trim to the top board must be done before assembling the framework and installing it. Fancy cuts and trim are added to the top board to create an effect that the straight boards alone cannot. This is optional and a matter of taste, of course, but take a look at what it might add before you rule it out.

The openings where the edge boards meet the top boards can be left simply squared off; but these cuts can add style to the shelves, even matching it to some degree with your style of furniture.

Some of the styles require that extra pieces of wood be added. Others are created by cutting the top board in a special way. A great number of variations is possible.

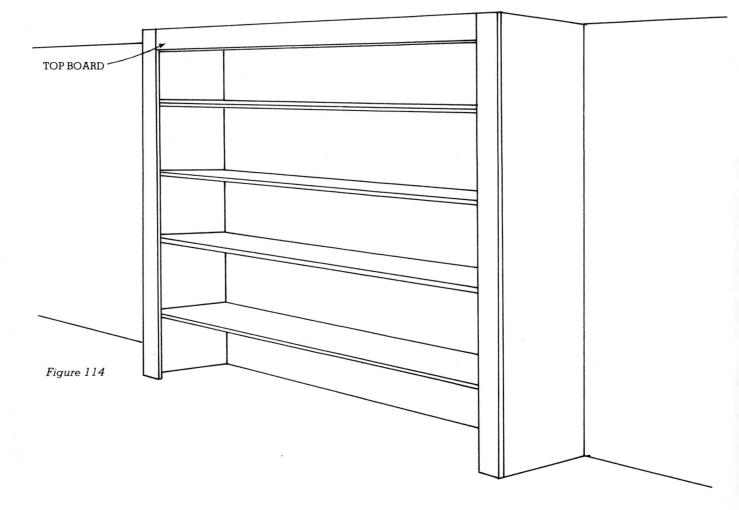

TOP BOARD

Figure 114

110

Figure 115 gives several ideas for such cutting and trim. Decorators' magazines and furniture catalogues will reveal many others.

Making a repeating pattern that is cut into a top board (or any board, for that matter) can be a little tricky. Here is a method for getting it right every time.

Once you have selected the pattern, separate it into its smallest segment that contains the complete design. Make a cardboard template of that segment out of shirt cardboard or other solid cardboard. (Corrugated cardboard like that found in boxes is not suitable for the template. The corrugations will make the pencil bounce as it is traced, leaving a wavy line.) (See Figure 116.)

Locate the center point of the top board and make a pencil line at that point. If you have a multi-element design (e.g., curves and points, as shown in Figure 116), decide if you want a curve or point

to fall in the center, or whatever element you want centered. Then, place your template so that it lines up properly and trace along it with a pencil. Now move the template to the left or right, match up the design, and trace the next segment. Continue doing this until the pattern is drawn across the entire board. It is now ready to cut.

If your design is cut from the top board, then once it is cut and sanded smooth, it is assembled with the edge boards and installed. If your design calls for pieces to be added, then install the top- and edge-board framework first and add the extras later.

If for some reason the top board does not sit exactly flush at the ceiling, a piece of fine trim wood (molding) nailed at the ceiling along the top board will mask all manner of gaps.

Behind this top board, by the way, is an ideal location to add concealed lighting. If this is part of your plan, look back to the "lighting" paragraphs of the "Planning and Design" section.

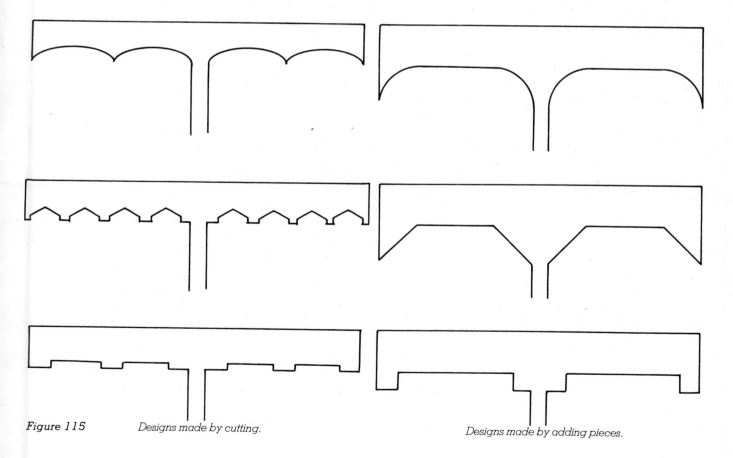

Figure 115   Designs made by cutting.   Designs made by adding pieces.

MAKING A WALL

By adding sides and front-trim pieces, your shelves will take on a built-in look. This look can be enhanced even further by building them from wall to wall, even (or possibly especially) if the wall has a door or a window in it.

The extra depth of the shelves gives the impression of a very thick wall. Build your shelves right up to the edge of the door or window and add a segment above it and below it in the case of the window.

Finishing these add-ons is the same as finishing the rest of the shelves. Clear finishes and paint are the two basic options.

Painting the shelves to match the woodwork in the room and painting the wall spaces between the shelves to match the rest of the walls can be very attractive and add interest to the shelf unit. This kind of treatment, as well as painting the shelves a contrasting color, will make the shelves stand out in the room.

On the other hand, if you want to play down the presence of the shelves, painting them all one color, preferably the same color as the rest of the room, will make them seem to recede or disappear in the room.

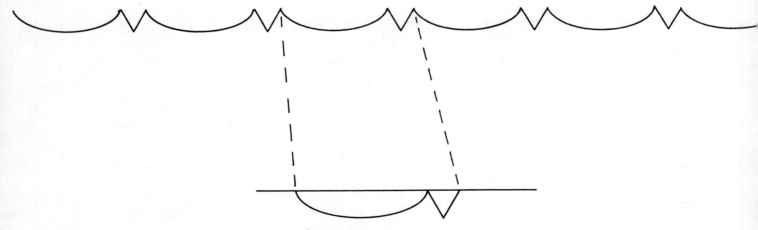

Figure 116

One complete design segment.

Doors

Note: Please read all the way through this section before beginning your doors. Choice of hardware and knowledge of how the doors are hung can affect your decisions—so get all the facts first.

* * *

Doors added to shelves basically serve two purposes: to hide the incredible mess on the shelves and to enhance the overall appearance of your shelf system. Some special-purpose doors can also serve as a bar, as we will see a little later. But mostly the doors make the shelves look like furniture, make them blend into the room decor and add interest to the units.

We'll take two avenues to getting doors for your shelves—doors you can buy and those you can build. Then, at the end of this section we'll cover how to install your doors.

A few general hints from the outset: When measuring the opening you want to fill with a door, a small amount of space must be allowed so that the doors will clear the surrounding areas and swing and open easily. Gaps of 1/8 inch on each side of the door are generally adequate, but don't be surprised if you find yourself doing a little trimming somewhere along the line. But if you do, take heart. It is far easier to trim the doors smaller than it is to trim them larger.

Doors for your shelves can be purchased. One easy source is building-supply stores. They carry both louver and solid doors that are used often as shutters on inside windows. They are available in a wide variety of sizes, some prefinished, some unfinished. Many times they'll have all the needed hardware installed or included. If not, it will be available nearby.

Another source for commercially available doors is from suppliers or distributors of kitchen cabinets.

Companies that specialize in remodeling kitchens may even give you some, although you should expect to have to do some work on them to make them usable, stripping paint at the least. Don't be put off by the fact that they are kitchen doors. Some of the best-looking doors available today are kitchen cabinet doors. They can be found in an astounding variety of styles.

The flea-market/garage-sale bonanza might also be a source. I have seen great doors on pieces of furniture headed for the junkyard. Usually I take the doors and discard the furniture if there is no usable wood in it. Probably these doors will be old, and so the wood will generally be of much higher quality than what is available today. But, as with the kitchen doors, you can expect to have some work to do before they are ready for your installation.

Lately I've been seeing a lot of imitations of old signs and mirrors in all kinds of stores. Some of these might be useful as doors, too.

Naturally, if you have a specific requirement, a cabinet maker can custom make the doors for you. This can be the most expensive, although satisfactory, solution.

BUILDING YOUR OWN DOORS

The construction of all the doors that follow is not difficult; but take care to make them precisely. The dividend of this attention will be doors that fit well, operate easily, and look good.

I'll cover three types of doors you can make and present them in what seems to me to be the order from easiest to most difficult. But even the most difficult door described is not beyond the reach of the amateur carpenter.

Flat sheet doors

The first type of door is a flat sheet of wood, plywood or hardwood. Solid pine is generally not suitable for this type of door because of its tendency to warp.

The piece is cut to size, leaving enough space for the hinge and clearance with other doors and uprights.

These flat doors can be attractive just as they are; or you can add a decorative touch by nailing small molding to the front of the door in a pattern. See Figure 118 for some trimming ideas.

Figure 117

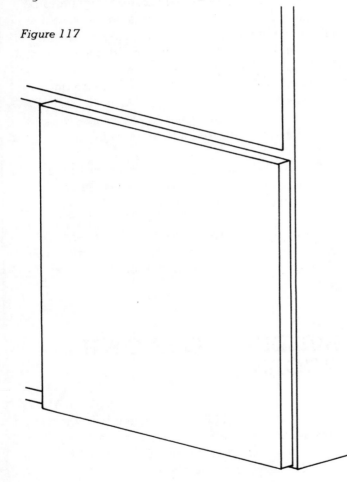

The molding can be stained or painted in a matching or contrasting color. The area enclosed by the molding can be covered with fabric, Contact paper, wall paper, découpage, or anything you dream up.

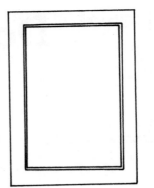 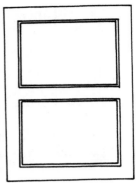

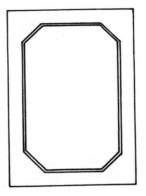 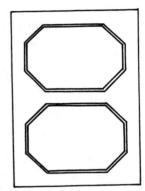

Figure 118

If your flat door is made from plywood, the inside area of the door can be cut out in just about any shape you might want. But be sure to leave at least 1-1/2 inches all around so that the door remains strong. More information about this type of door is given in the paragraphs under "Frame Doors" a little later on in this section.

Tongue-and-groove doors

The second type of build-it-yourself door I call tongue-and-groove doors. These consist of pieces of tongue-and-groove wood like pine planks, or hardwood flooring fastened together with cleats. Tongue-and-groove wood generally comes in widths between 2 and 3 inches. The cleats are made from leftover tongue and groove or from 1 by 2's. See Figure 119 for the exact construction.

It will probably be necessary to trim down the door somewhat. If you have enough to be trimmed, cut the tongue off one edge and the lips of the

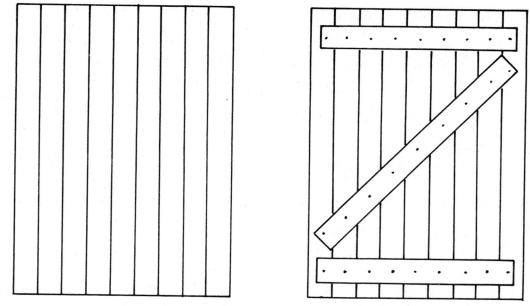

Figure 119 Either side can be the front of the door.

groove off the other. If there is not that much to be trimmed, trim the tongue off one end so that you will have a smooth and flat surface to screw the hinges into.

Frame doors

The third type of door I'll refer to as frame doors. These consist of a frame made of 1 by 2's (or 1 by 3's) and an insert of some kind. There are two ways that the frame can be constructed.

The first is by simply butting the frame pieces along their edges, the vertical pieces running from top to bottom, the horizontal pieces fitting in between the vertical pieces.

Fastening the pieces together can be done with long wood screws (see Figure 121) or by using dowels in place of the screws. Steel flat corners can also be used with satisfactory results; however, they will not hold the joints together as tightly as the screws or dowels glued in place.

The second frame construction technique is mitering. The frame pieces are cut carefully at a 45-degree angle either by hand or by hand using a mitre box. The mitre box is preferable since it will ensure accurate cuts.

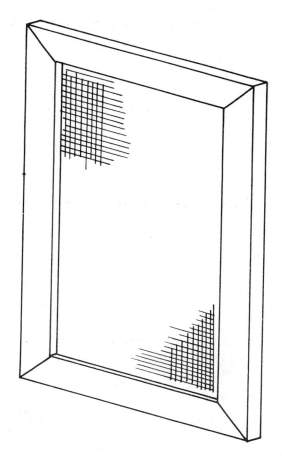

Figure 120 Frame door.

To assemble, check the fit of the parts; a little sanding or wood filler will cover a multitude of small errors. As with the butted frames, wood screws, glued dowels, or flat corners can be used. Again, flat corners are the least likely to produce tight joints.

And now that you have an open frame, you'll want to fill it in with something. There are many ways to complete the frame door. Here I'll suggest a few practical options rather than attempt an exhaustive list.

A solid filling can be made simply by tacking a thin piece of plywood or other wood right across the back of the frame. This piece of wood can be stained or painted to match or contrast with the front; or it can be covered with fabric, wall paper, you name it.

Cane and rattan weaves are now available on machine-made rolls that look as good as if an Old World craftsman spent 20 hours on each piece. These can be stapled to the back of the frame.

A more ambitious way to complete the project is to make stained-glass inserts for the doors. Virtually every hobby shop carries kits and supplies for stained glass.

Lattice, like what roses grow on, can also be used. It is made from small strips of lumber available pre-cut for just that purpose from the lumberyard. Figure 122 shows how to put it together.

Figure 121

Small blocks of lattice are added along the sides to makes these sit flat. Nail each strip in place with a small nail at each end.

Figure 122

You can also use window glass or Plexiglass. The plexi can be clear, smoked, or colored, smooth or textured. For glass (like some other types of inserts), fitting the material into the opening of the frame and securing it with small trim molding on both sides is the best way to complete the job.

One last suggestion: speaker-grill cloth. Available at electronic supply houses, this comes in a wide variety of weaves, colors, and designs. It is a must if you plan to conceal speakers behind the doors and wish to have music with the doors closed. Speaker-grill cloth is made so that sound will pass right through it and not be muffled.

HANGING THE DOORS

Hanging the completed doors is next. There are three basic ways to hang the doors: flush, overlapping, and drop-down. Figure 123 illustrates these.

The method you choose for hanging your doors will determine what type of hinges you will use and how you will attach them. Figure 124 shows the different types and how they are installed.

Flat-butt hinges are the easiest to use and are relatively easy to conceal. A continuous-butt hinge (also called a piano hinge), although requiring more screws to install, is the strongest of these hinges. It will hold its alignment best, especially if you expect to subject it to heavy use.

The offset-butt hinges are designed for specific uses, mostly with overlapping doors. If you have a specific application for a hinge not shown, chances are better than 50/50 that someone makes it. Check with a good hardware supply store.

Concealing the hinges is done by "mortising" them, that is, by recessing them into the wood. The wood is chipped away by using a chisel. You do this by cutting a line about 1/8-inch deep all the way around the border of the hinge and then chipping away the wood inside the line.

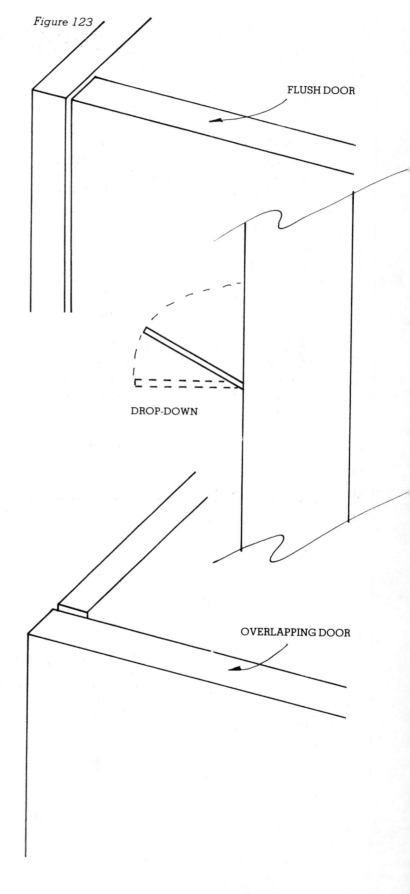

Figure 123

FLUSH DOOR

DROP-DOWN

OVERLAPPING DOOR

Although hiding the hinges and other hardware is often desirable, decorative hardware can be an asset to the appearance of the finished unit. Decorative hinges and door pulls are available in chrome, wrought iron (black), hammered copper, and polished brass.

The doors, when they are closed, will need to rest against a stop of some sort. This stop can be a cleat made of wood that stands vertically where the door will stop, or might be a friction or magnetic catch similar to those used on kitchen doors (Fig. 125).

A tip for successful door hanging: First attach the hinge to the door itself; then, while resting the door on three or four paper matches, screw the hinge to the shelf unit. Pilot holes for all screws will make your job easier.

Another method for hanging the doors is to make them so they drop down. In its lowered (open) position, a drop-down door becomes an extension of the shelf. Such doors are particularly useful in a situation where a shelf extension is helpful in removing items from the shelves.

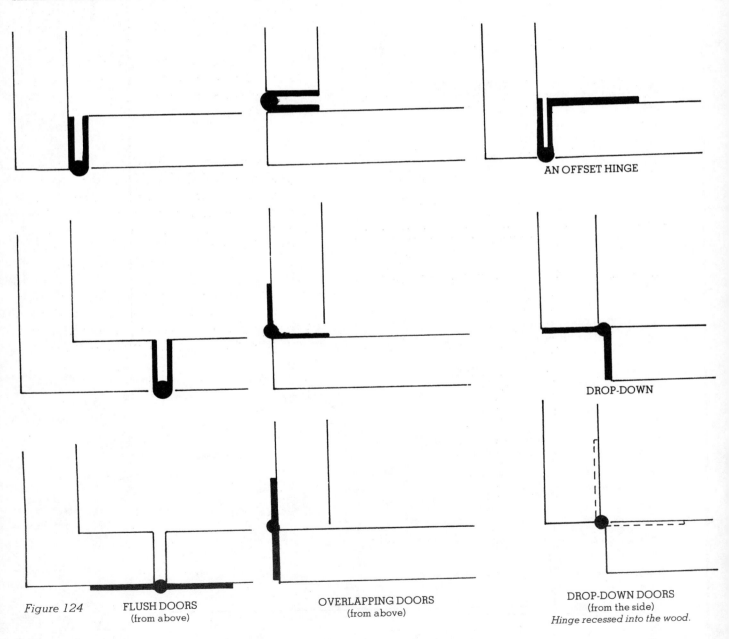

AN OFFSET HINGE

DROP-DOWN

Figure 124   FLUSH DOORS
(from above)

OVERLAPPING DOORS
(from above)

DROP-DOWN DOORS
(from the side)
Hinge recessed into the wood.

118

A drop-down door of this type (like the fold-down tables covered in the next section) can also serve as a bar surface. If you plan this use, a thin sheet of cork applied to the door inside will provide a non-slip, water-tolerant surface. The cork is fastened with contact cement.

Drop-down doors can be made in any of the ways mentioned earlier. The difference between these and the other doors is that the allowance for the hinge to clear must be made from top to bottom rather than from side to side.

Piano hinges are best for this type of door because of the weight they might have to carry. In addition to the hinge, a special piece of hardware called a stay support is used. As shown in Figure 126, this holds the door in a horizontal position.

The stay support is installed after the door is in place. The door is supported so that it is level (parallel to the floor) and the location of the stay support is marked with a pencil. The stay support is then fastened to the door with the screws provided and, with the door held level, it is fastened to the upright.

You may need one or two stay supports. The decision is made based upon the size of the door and the weight it will have to carry in its open position. If the door is wider than 36 inches, definitely use two. If you have any concern about weight, also use two.

A friction or magnetic catch holds the door in its up position. If one catch seems insufficient to hold it, add a second catch of the same type. The friction type generally holds better than the magnetic.

TIP A trick you can use to hold the door level is to make a strap of fiber-glass strapping tape and allow that to hold the door while you drive the screws. As always, pilot holes speed the job.

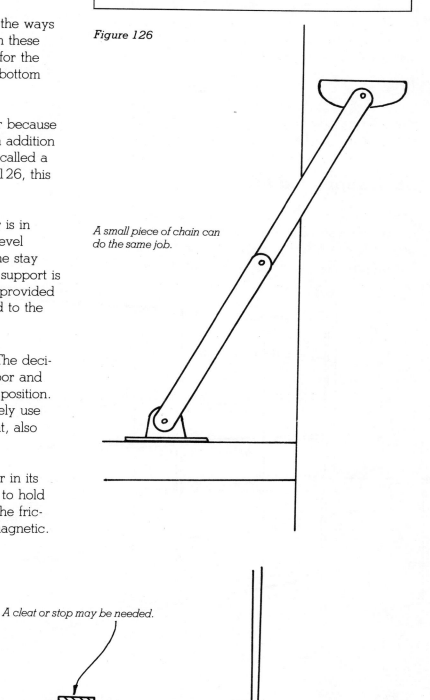

Figure 126

A small piece of chain can do the same job.

Figure 125

A cleat or stop may be needed.

119

Tables

Tables which lift up or drop down have many uses, depending on what room the shelves are in. They can be used as dining tables, desks, drawing boards, dressing tables, a bar, a work bench, virtually anythng you can imagine.

These tables will fall into two categories: those that get all their support from the shelves, and those that are supported at one end by the shelves and the other end by leg.

Shelf-supported tables

The tables that get all their support from the shelves are easy to make. They consist of a piece of 3/4-inch-thick wood (plywood, particle board, or hardwood). The maximum width of the table is the same as the distance between two uprights. The maximum depth I recommend for these tables is 3 feet. The reason for this limit is that the stress put on the hinge and shelves due to leverage of a deeper shelf would be too great for a table of greater depth.

The table top is attached to a shelf using piano hinge or flush counter hinges. If you choose the flush counter hinges, you must recess them into the wood. This is done with a chisel, removing enough wood so that the hinge will be flush with the top. Take your time with this, making small bites with the chisel. The area where you have chipped away the wood may be somewhat rough, but the hinge covers it. (See Fig. 128.)

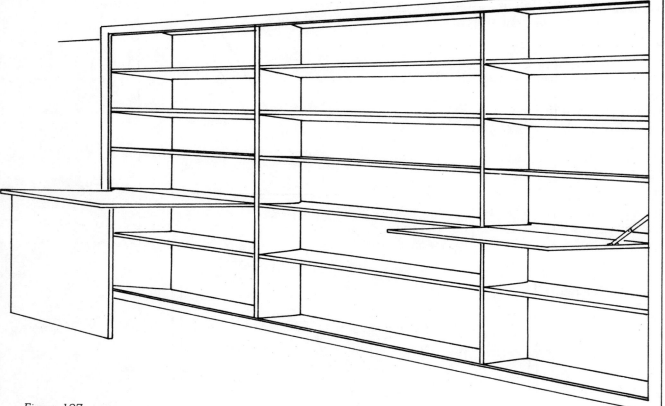

Figure 127

These tables can either drop down or lift up, depending on your preference.

The only difference in making and installing these is the placement of the hinges and other hardware. When the table drops down, all the hardware is on the top side. When the table lifts up, all the hardware is underneath the table top.

Both the drop-down and lift-up tables require some sort of extra hardware to hold them level when they are in the open position. For the drop-down table, a small piece of chain will do nicely. You can also use a stay support (see Fig. 129). This is attached to the table top and one upright (as shown). If the table will carry a lot of weight or get very heavy use, consider using two supports.

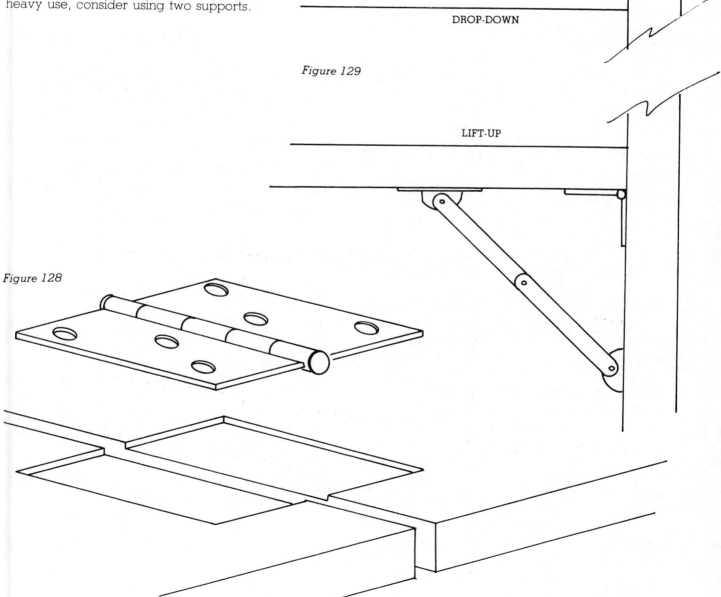

STAY SUPPORT OR CHAIN

DROP-DOWN

Figure 129

LIFT-UP

Figure 128

The lift-up table is held in its open position with a stay support which is installed under it. The position of the support stay on the lift-up table is more critical than on the drop-down table, so mark its location carefully.

Tables with extra support

If you want your table to be deeper than 3 feet, an extra leg is a must to keep the table from sagging or pulling the shelves over. There are three ways in which this can be accomplished. The first and easiest is to make the extra leg permanent, such that the table is always down. The second and third ways still allow the table to fold up. One method conceals the leg entirely when the table is in the up position; the other allows the leg to hang on the outside of the table when it is up.

In building these, the table top will attach to the shelves in the same manner as the shelf-supported ones. The extra legs are attached to the tops.

7/8"). The hinge is placed so that the end of the leg rests squarely on the underside of the top. A stay support is used to keep the leg from collapsing under the table. You can use one or two of these, depending on the type of use the table will get. If you are in doubt, use two.

The "invisible" leg, that is, the leg that is hidden when the table is in the up position, pivots on a special hinge that you make yourself from a "flat corner," a piece of metal available in any hardware store.

The flat corner attaches solidly to the leg with wood screws. If the leg is made of plywood, the screws must be driven into the edge grain of the plywood, so be sure you drill pilot holes (Figure 14) so that the screw does not split the laminations apart. One of these flat corners is installed on each side of the leg. Use No. 6 or No. 8 wood screws that are at least 1-1/4 to 1-1/2 inches in length so that a firm grip is established.

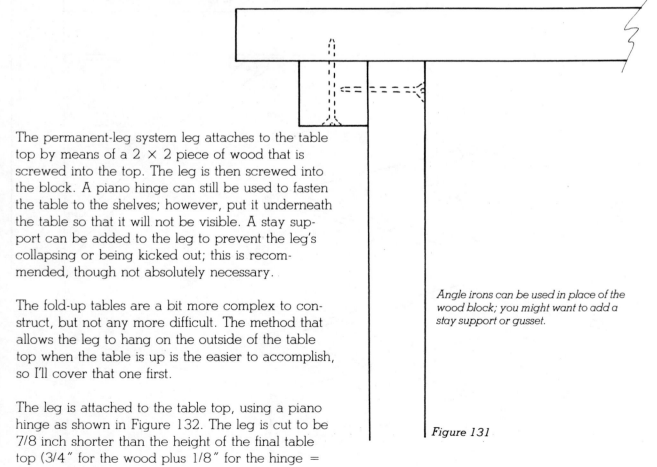

The permanent-leg system leg attaches to the table top by means of a 2 × 2 piece of wood that is screwed into the top. The leg is then screwed into the block. A piano hinge can still be used to fasten the table to the shelves; however, put it underneath the table so that it will not be visible. A stay support can be added to the leg to prevent the leg's collapsing or being kicked out; this is recommended, though not absolutely necessary.

The fold-up tables are a bit more complex to construct, but not any more difficult. The method that allows the leg to hang on the outside of the table top when the table is up is the easier to accomplish, so I'll cover that one first.

The leg is attached to the table top, using a piano hinge as shown in Figure 132. The leg is cut to be 7/8 inch shorter than the height of the final table top (3/4" for the wood plus 1/8" for the hinge =

Angle irons can be used in place of the wood block; you might want to add a stay support or gusset.

Figure 131

The illustration (Figure 133) shows that a screw in the flat-corner side that is attached to the table top becomes a pivot point for the leg. Since this pivot point is the point of greatest stress on the unit, a special treatment will be needed for it.

Figure 134 illustrates how this is done. A 3/4-inch hole is drilled in the plywood as shown. A nut and bolt is used to fasten the flat corner to the top, passing through another hole drilled through the edge and into the 3/4-inch hole.

A flat washer is put between the flat corner and the top of the table to help the leg pivot more smoothly.

The 3/4-inch hole left behind is plugged using two pieces of 3/4-inch dowel, one on each side of the hole. They will need to be cut rather thin and glued in place. They are sanded flush with the top and finished along with it.

The edges of the plywood should be filled with wood filler and sanded smooth before finishing. If you plan on using a clear finish, veneer tape (very thin strips of wood with an adhesive backing) can be applied to the edges. This makes the legs and top appear as if they are solid wood and gives a neat, professional-looking result.

The almost limitless usability of these tables in your shelf system makes them worthy of your serious consideration. Don't shy away from them because of their relative complexity; the results will be worth the work.

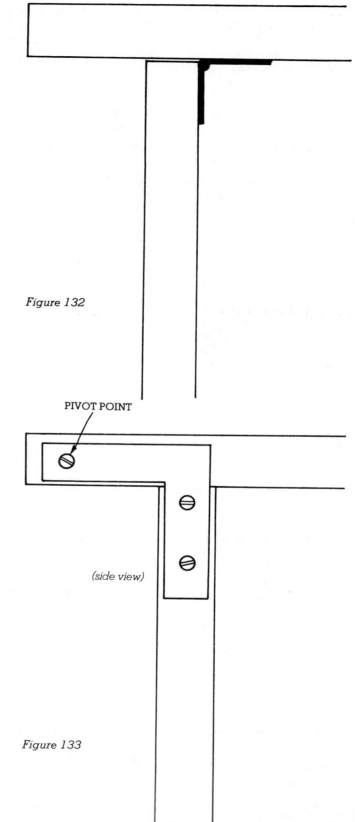

Figure 132

PIVOT POINT

(side view)

Figure 133

Figure 134

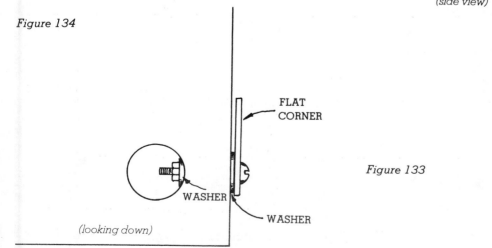

FLAT CORNER

WASHER

WASHER

(looking down)

A Bed

Add a bed to a set of shelves? Why not? For a guest room, or a kids' room (the occasional overnighter is inevitable), or even as a child's permanent bed. These fold-down beds, a variation of the old Murphy bed, have many advantages. They leave maximum floor space in the room when not in use, and when closed up they can conceal some of the mess. They make an attractive, practical, and relatively easy addition to build.

A standard single mattress measures about 73 inches long by 36 inches wide, so that will be our size guideline. However, since a regular mattress can be bulky and heavy, consider using a 3- or 4-inch-thick piece of foam instead. These are easy and inexpensive to buy, lightweight, and quite comfortable. And since the bed will be lifted up and down, the savings in weight will be meaningful.

The bedboard should be made from 3/4-inch plywood. To eliminate the need for extra framework or bracing, add 2 or 3 drop-down feet to support the bed. This will also take some of the strain off the shelves, particularly when the inevitable pillow fight breaks out.

There are two ways the bed can be arranged to drop down—along its length or across its width. Consider using the one that drops down along its length if the bed is for a child, since this style requires the least amount of leverage and effort to put back up.

The differences in putting the two beds together involve only minor details since the construction techniques for both are the same. Piano hinges (available up to 6 feet long) will do the bulk of the work. The bed itself will hinge on one as will each of the legs.

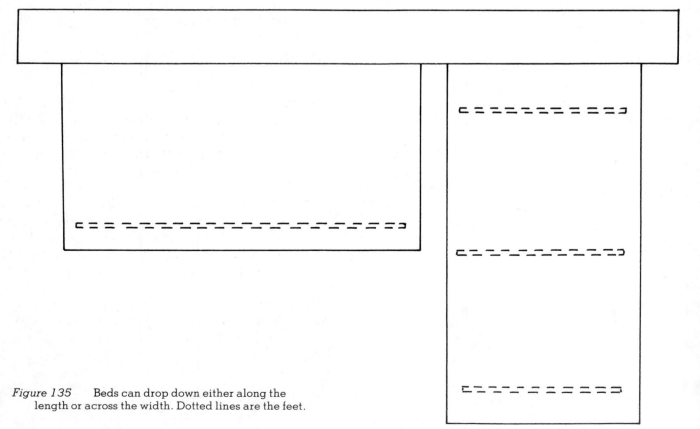

Figure 135   Beds can drop down either along the
        length or across the width. Dotted lines are the feet.

The bed is attached to a secure shelf or to a 2 × 4 fastened along the front of the shelf unit specifically for the bed to attach to. The height of the bed should be kept to within 12 to 18 inches off the floor; this will allow the legs to be attached to the back side of the bedboard without their having to overlap. The bedboard is fastened in place with a full-length piano hinge along the length or width of the board, depending on how you are arranging your bed.

The drop-down legs are made of 3/4-inch plywood or particle board and are cut to the same height as the bed less 7/8 inch (3/4 inch for the thickness of the bedboard plus 1/8 inch for the hinges). The legs are also hinged along their entire length with piano hinges. Figure 136 shows the correct way to install the hinges. Use screws that will not poke through the wood. Three of these legs, arranged as shown in Figure 136, are needed for the bed that drops down along its width; one or two are needed for the bed that drops down along its length.

All legs should be inset at least 3 inches from any edge to lower the risk of kicking them. There is nothing I hate more than kicking a bed leg barefoot in the middle of the night.

When the bed is folded up, it is attached at the top using hooks and eyes. The illustration (Figure 137) gives one suggestion for placing them.

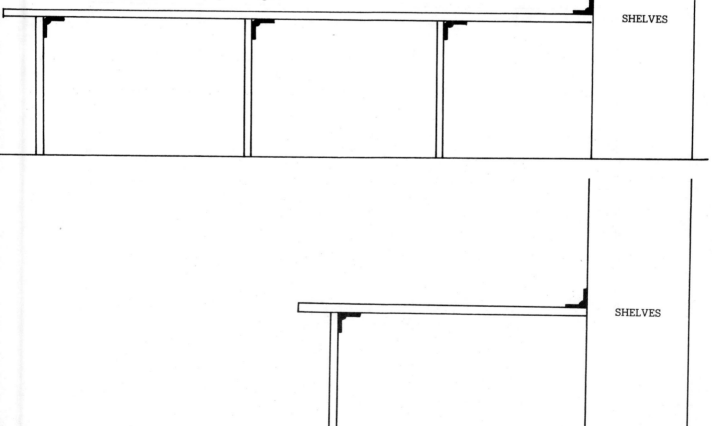

SHELVES

SHELVES

Figure 136

Care must be taken in using the wood blocks or hooks and eyes to see that they are installed securely—no surprises for junior playing under the bed, OK?

The foam mattress can be removed and stored away if the need for it is only occasional. However, it can also be secured to the bedboard if it will be used daily and if there is enough space behind the board in the up position. The securing of the foam is done with strips of sheet about 4 inches wide, folded in half lengthwise and stapled on either side of the mattress. Two of these strips are usually enough; they will not interfere with the comfort of the sleeper.

Care should be taken when finishing these beds, particularly if they are for use by children, to make sure that all places where splinters could be picked up are sanded smooth.

The unit can be finished in any of the ways described in the section on "Planning and Design." An idea you might consider if the bed is built in a child's room for guest use is to make the mattress removable and paint a little village with roads, etc., on the bedboard. The kids will love to push cars and trucks around on it, and toy animals take well to it, too.

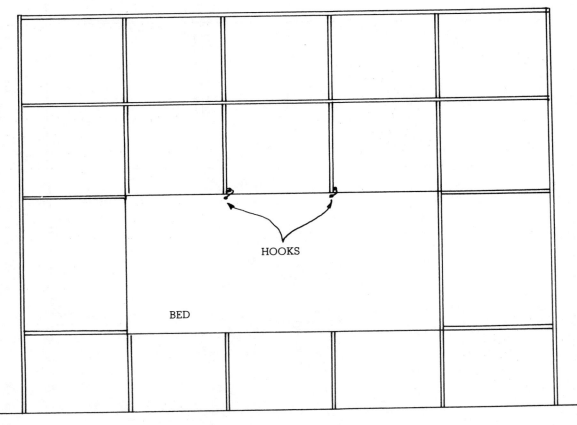

HOOKS

BED

Figure 137

Part Six
Appendix

Glossary of Terms

The terms included here appear in the text and have been defined in order to clarify their use in context. Most of the words that have been defined here also have other meanings; so for a complete understanding of each, it may be necessary to consult a dictionary. And, since further information about the application of these terms will be found in the text, consult the fine index at the back of the book.

anchor (1) A device for holding something firmly, including fasteners for hollow walls and masonry. Anchors are designated by the materials they are made from, e.g., lead anchor, plastic anchor, etc. (2) To affix or fasten firmly.

angle iron A piece of iron or steel that is bent to a 90-degree angle, used to hold up shelves or reinforce corners. Angle irons have pre-drilled holes in them for screws or bolts.

back, backing A piece or pieces of wood fastened to the back of a set of shelves to improve strength or prevent racking.

beam A piece of wood or metal used to support something, usually a ceiling or floor.

bin A container with an open top used for storage.

brace An angular support used to hold something in place or keep it steady. See also *bracket.*

bracket A specially-made piece of wood or metal used to hold up a shelf.

butt joint A method of joining two pieces of wood by placing the end or edge of one against the surface of the other and nailing or screwing them together.

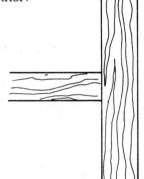

butterfly See *toggle bolt.*

chisel A tool with a sharp blade at the end of a strong shaft. Used to cut or shape wood and other materials.

clamp (1) An adjustable device for temporarily holding two or more objects firmly together. (2) To use a clamp to hold two or more things together.

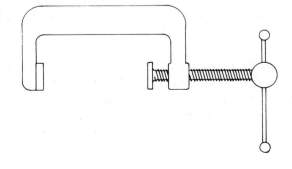

clothes bar   The metal or wood bar in a closet that the clothes hangers hang on.

composition board   A wood sheet made of chips or flakes of wood mixed with sawdust and a bonding material, all pressed and heated to make it solid. Also called particle board or flake board.

construction grade   The lowest grade of wood, cut and left in its rough-cut form.

coping saw   A thin-bladed saw with a deep frame used for cutting curves.

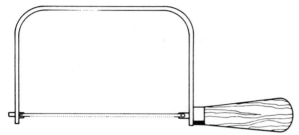

crutch tip   A rubber cup that covers the end of a rod or dowel to protect or cushion another surface.

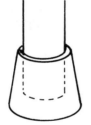

dado joint   A method of fastening two pieces of wood together whereby a groove is cut in one piece of wood to accept the end or edge of the other.

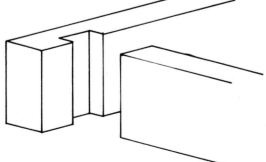

dowel   A round wooden rod. Dowel diameters range from 1/8 inch to 1-1/2 inches.

drill   A tool for spinning a drill bit. There are hand-operated and electric drills.

drill bit   A cutting tool for making holes. Drill bits come in many diameters and in many types, such as twist drills and butterfly bits.

drywall   A plaster-like material formed into a sheet and coated on both sides with a paper material. Used for interior walls. Drywall is so named because it is put up dry; plaster, on the other hand, is mixed with water and put up wet. Also know as plasterboard.

emery cloth   A type of abrasive paper made with a cloth backing covered with very fine chips of emery, a hard black mineral used for polishing.

fender washer   A washer with a wider shoulder and smaller hole than a regular washer.

FENDER WASHER   REGULAR WASHER

fiber glass strapping tape   A type of adhesive-backed tape in which long strands of fiber glass have been embedded to make the tape difficult to tear or break.

file   (1) A steel tool with small grooves or teeth in it. Used for smoothing or shaping. (2) To use a file to smooth or shape.

finger-tight   A slang term referring to the degree of tightness that results from tightening something (e.g., a nut-and-bolt) as much as possible using only your fingers.

fitting   A special part used to hold pieces of pipe together, to split one pipe into two, etc.

flake board   See *composition board*.

flange   A metal plate with a projecting collar, used to hold a pipe or other object in place.

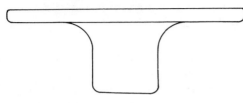

free-standing   Requiring no external support.

galvanize   To cover metal, usually steel, with a coating of zinc to prevent rust.

gusset   A triangular piece of wood, metal, etc., fastened across two perpendicular surfaces to add strength or resistance to racking.

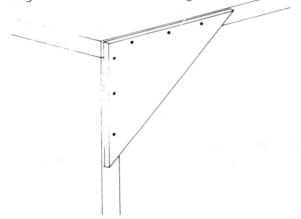

hacksaw   A metal-bladed saw with small teeth for cutting metals.

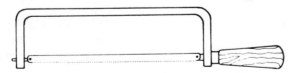

hardboard   A type of composition board. See *Masonite*.

hardwood   Generally, very dense wood with tightly packed grain; it is very difficult to dent or mar. Wood coming from trees with leaves as opposed to needles, e.g., oak, walnut, cherry, mahogany, maple, teak, and others.

hat shelf   The shelf above the clothes bar in a closet; traditionally used for storing hats.

hinge   A flexible or movable joint on which a door, cover, gate, or lid moves.

hollow door   A door made with a strong outer frame and a thin wood or metal covering on each side.

jig saw   See *sabre saw*.

joint   A place where two things come together, i.e., two pieces of wood, pipe, etc.

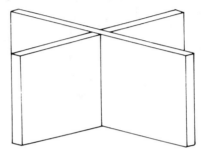

joist   Wood beams (2 x 6, 2 x 8, 2 x 10, etc.) that hold up a ceiling and support the floor above.

judgement call   A sports phrase that describes a situation in which an occurrence could be called by the referee in either of two ways i.e., really just a matter of opinion. I have used it in reference to a situation that could be treated equally well in either of two ways, such that one's opinion would make the difference.

kick-plate   A coined term used to describe a piece of wood or metal that is installed at floor level for the sake of appearance and for protection from kicks.

laminate   (1) A thin sheet (e.g., wood veneer) glued or fastened to another material. Formica is a trademark for a plastic laminate. (2) To build something up layer by layer, or to apply a thin layer of material like wood, etc., on top of another material.

lamination   An individual layer of a multi-layered piece of wood.

level (1) A tool for determining if something is parallel to the horizontal plane, or perpendicular to the vertical plane. (2) Even or flat, parallel to the ground or floor. (3) To adjust something to make it even or flat or parallel to the ground or floor.

liquor box method A coined phrase describing pieces of wood put together by cutting slots in each; also called "cross lap."

load The amount of weight or stress on a shelf.

mallet A special type of hammer with a head made from a material softer than steel, e.g., rubber, wood, plastic, or leather.

Masonite® A trademark for a type of hardboard made of tiny wood fibres pressed and heated to form sheets. Also referred to as hardboard.

milling The trimming of rough-cut lumber to its final size and smoothness.

miter (1) A right-angle joint made by cutting the ends of two pieces of wood at 45 degrees. (2) To make such a joint.

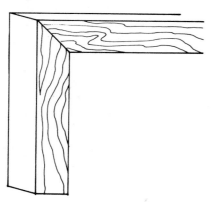

miter box A saw guide for cutting a miter.

molding Strips of wood used for trim or decoration, commonly found in a wide variety of sizes and shapes in lumberyards.

Molly Fastener® A trademark (of The Molly Co., USM Corp., Reading, Pa.) for a special fastening bolt used for attaching materials to hollow walls. The sleeve of this fastener expands behind the wall to get a firm grip. Known commonly as a molly bolt. (See section "Fastening and Hanging" in Part I.)

nail set A small, pointed tool for pushing finishing (headless) nails below the surface of the wood.

nailing strip A strip of wood installed against a wall, floor, or some other piece of wood so that another piece (e.g., shelf) can rest on it and/or be fastened to it.

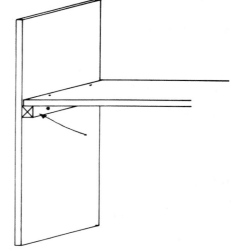

O.D. Stands for outer diameter.

particle board See *composition board*.

peg system A system for holding up shelves by the support of small pegs that fit into holes in the uprights.

pilot bit A special tool for making pilot holes.

pilot hole A drilled hole that is smaller than the shank diameter of the wood screw to be used in it. The pilot hole eases the way for a screw by removing some of the material that the screw would have otherwise had to pass through, yet leaves enough material for the screw to get a solid grip. A pilot hole makes driving screws easier and lessens the chances of splitting or cracking the material.

plaster A cement-like material that is mixed with water and applied as a wall covering and smoother. Plaster is usually applied over thin wood strips called lath.

plasterboard   See *drywall*.

plastic anchor   A special fastener that is installed in a hole in plaster or drywall to hold a screw more securely than if the screw were driven into the plaster without it.

Plexiglas®   The Rohm and Hass trademark for acrylic plastic formed into sheets, rods, etc.

plow   To cut a groove in wood.

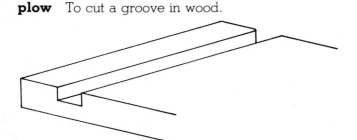

plumb line   A string with a weight on one end. When allowed to hang freely, it will give a visual reference for checking whether something is exactly vertical.

polyurethane   A clear finish made from a special plastic (polyurethane) dissolved in a volatile liquid, usually a mineral spirits derivative. Nearly indestructible.

PVC   Stands for polyvinyl chloride, a plastic material used for making plastic pipe. It also comes in sheets and other forms.

rabbet joint   A joint formed by cutting a groove on a surface or along the edge of a piece of wood so that another piece of wood (or other material) will fit into it.

racking   The tendency of a shelf unit to sway from side to side.

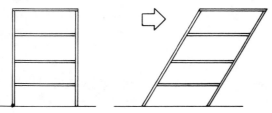

radial arm saw   A power saw with a circular blade suspended above a table. The saw can be moved forward and back as well as pivoted from side to side.

router   A high-speed power tool for cutting a rabbet or dado joint or other similar, special cuts.

runs   A slide or ramp for storing canned goods.

sabre saw   A small electric saw with a blade that moves up and down. It can be used to cut along straight or curved lines.

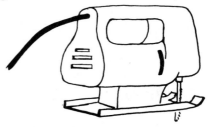

sag   The tendency of a material to bend under pressure or weight.

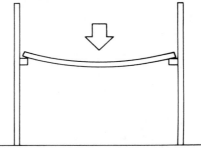

set screw   A screw which is used to hold or "set" an object in place. A flange will often have a set screw as part of it to hold a pipe in place.

screw eye   A metal eye on a shank with threads (similar to a wood screw).

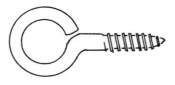

scriber   A sharply pointed, pencil-like tool used for scratching a line into metals, plastics, and other materials. A glass cutter is an example of a scriber for glass. There are special scribers for different materials.

shelf A horizontal, flat piece of wood, metal, plastic, glass, etc., used to store or display things.

shellac A clear finish made by dissolving a special resin in alcohol. Alcohol, ammonia, or detergent, if spilled on a surface that has been shellacked, will spoil the finish.

softwood Wood that comes from evergreen trees like pine, fir, spruce, and cedar. Softwood fibers are less tightly packed together than those of hardwood, making surface penetration easier.

sole plate The metal plate that forms the bottom of an electric saw and upon which it rides while cutting. Also called a "shoe."

solvent (welding solvent) A chemical substance which melts Plexiglas. A strong joint results as two pieces are welded or melted together.

standard A piece of metal or wood which, when attached to a solid surface, is used to hold up shelf supports.

stay-support A piece of hardware that holds a table or door at a 90-degree angle to another surface.

strip heater A long, thin, electric heating element enclosed in an insulating wrapping. Used to heat and soften Plexiglas along the line of an intended bend.

stud A vertical wood support (usually a 2 × 4)

that forms the inside of a wall and to which the wall covering is nailed.

stud finder A hand-held tool with a free-moving magnetic needle. Nails used to fasten the wall covering to the studs will attract the magnetic needle, thus revealing where the studs are.

support A wood or metal bracket that attaches to a standard to hold up a shelf.

sway To move from side to side.

system (1) Two or more units of shelves put together to make a more complex or larger area of shelves; e.g., wall system. (2) A method of building or assembling a set of shelves; e.g., the "pipe system."

"S" hook A piece of strong metal wire bent into an "S" shape that is used for joining two pieces of chain together; it has other similar applications.

table saw An electric saw with a circular blade that extends up from below a table.

thick wall *or* **thin wall** Descriptive terms used in reference to the thickness of the material that pipe or tubing is made of.

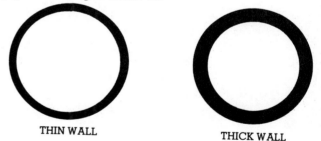

THIN WALL   THICK WALL

thumb nut See *wing nut.*

toggle bolt A special fastener for use in plaster or drywall; it consists of a long bolt with a special nut having wings that open behind the wall.

unit An assembly consisting of two uprights supporting one or more shelves.

upright The vertical support for a shelf or shelves.

varnish   A clear finish made by dissolving a special resin in oil or turpentine or other volatile liquid. Varnish is not harmed by alcohol, ammonia, water, or detergents.

warp   To bend or twist out of shape. In wood, warping is caused by improper drying or excessive moisture, and improper storage.

"wet or dry" sandpaper   Sandpaper with extremely fine grit that can be used with water or without. Water is used to wash the sanding dust out of the paper, and thus prevents the paper from becoming too clogged.

wing nut   A nut with "ears" attached to it so that it can be tightened or loosened with the fingers.

zinc plated   Also called galvanizing, a thin coating that is electroplated on steel or iron to help prevent rust.

Sources of Additional Information

MATERIALS

Wood

The American Plywood Association
1119 A Street
Tacoma, Washington 98401

Georgia Pacific
900 S.W. Fifth Avenue
Portland, Oregon 97204

Weyerhaeuser Corporation
P.O. Box 1188
Chesapeake, Virginia 23320

Woodcraft Supply Corporation
313 Montvale Avenue
Woburn, Massachusetts 01801

Finishing

Homer Formby
P.O. Box 788
Olive Branch, Mississippi 38654

Closet accessories and hardware for shelving

Kirsch Company
309 N. Prospect Street
Sturgis, Mississippi 39769

Knape and Vogt Manufacturing Co.
2700 Oak Industrial Drive
Grand Rapids, Michigan 49505

Spacebuilder Closet Accessories
Closet Maid Corporation
720 W. 17th Street
Ocala, Florida 32670

Spacemaster Home Products Division
2501 N. Elaton Avenue
Chicago, Illinois 60647

Plexiglas

Rohm and Hass Company
P.O. Box 14619
Philadelphia, Pennsylvania 19134

Lighting

Halo Lighting Division
400 Busse Road
Elk Grove Village, Illinois 60007

Lightolier Corporation
346 Claremont Avenue
Jersey City, New Jersey 07305

Acrylic contact cement

Elmer's Information Center
P.O. Box 9817
St. Paul, Minnesota 55198

BOOKS

The Apartment Carpenter
by Howard Fink
New York: Quick Fox, Inc., 1977

Basic Carpentry Illustrated
Sunset Books
Menlo Park, California: Lane Publishing Co., 1976

The Complete Book of Woodwork
by Charles Haywood
New York: Drake Publishers, Inc., 1974

How to Paint Anything
by Hubbard H. Cobb
New York: Stein & Day Publishers, 1972

How To Use Power & Hand Tools
by George Daniels
New York: Barnes & Noble Books, 1974

How To Work With Tools and Wood
by Campbell Mager
New York: Pocket Books, 1975

Illustrated Basic Carpentry
by Graham Blackburn
Boston: Little, Brown & Company, 1976

*Know-How: A Fit-It Book for the Clumsy but Pure
        of Heart*
by Alland, Waskin, and Hiss
Boston: Little, Brown & Company, 1975

Modern Carpentry
by Willis H. Wagner
South Holland, Illinois: Goodheart-Willcox
        Company, 1976

New Complete Wood-Working Handbook
by Jannette T. Adams
New York: Arco Publishing Co., Inc., 1976

*Shop Tactics: The Common-Sense Way of Using
        Tools and Working with Woods, Metals, Plastic,
        and Glass*
by William Abler
Philadelphia: Running Press, 1976

*Staining & Finishing Unfinished Furniture and Other
        Naked Woods*
by George Grotz
New York: Doubleday & Company, 1973

The Wall Book
by Stanley Shuler
New York: M. Evans & Co., Inc., 1974

Wally's Workshop
by Wally Bruner
New York: Simon & Schuster, Inc., 1973

Index

Index

Note: A lowercase "a" following a page number (e.g., 16a) refers to the left-hand column of the page; "b" refers to the right. Page references in *italics* indicate that an illustration accompanies the indexed item.